THE
ONLY THING
THAT
MATTERS

Life has a reason and a purpose.
All people yearn to know what it is.
Most have not yet clearly understood.

We have been told that humanity's
Basic Instinct is survival.
That is not our Basic Instinct at all.

THE
ONLY THING
THAT
MATTERS

Book 2 in the

CONVERSATIONS with HUMANITY

Series

NEALE DONALD WALSCH

an *EmNin* book

Copyright © 2012 by Neale Donald Walsch

Published in the United States by: Emnin Books, 324 Wimer St.,
Ashland, OR 97520 • emninbooks@aol.com

Distributed in the United States by: Hay House, Inc.: www.hayhouse.com®

Published and distributed in Australia by: Hay House Australia Pty. Ltd.:
www.hayhouse.com.au • *Published and distributed in the United Kingdom by:* Hay House UK, Ltd.:
www.hayhouse.co.uk • *Published and distributed in the Republic of South Africa by:* Hay House
SA (Pty), Ltd.: www.hayhouse.co.za • *Distributed in Canada by:* Raincoast: www.raincoast.com •
Published in India by: Hay House Publishers India: www.hayhouse.co.in

Cover and interior design by: Frame25 Productions

Library of Congress Control Number: 2012945053

ISBN: 978-1-4019-4185-7
Digital ISBN: 978-1-4019-4186-4

16 15 14 13   8 7 6 5
1st edition, October 2012
5th edition, September 2013

Printed in the United States of America

This book is dedicated to Em Claire, the American poet whose voice has brought an end to loneliness and a new level of feeling, insight, clarity, honesty, and beauty to thousands of people around the world. I am thankful for the gifts she has given to us all, and to me, in a special, life-changing, and heart-stopping way, as my dearest friend, my wife, and, truly, my Other.

Part One

Four short conversations
beginning a longer exploration
that you have been yearning
to undertake for quite some time.

1

Your Soul Knows Exactly What It Is Doing

DEAR COMPANION ON THE JOURNEY: It is wonderful that you have come here.

There is something you wish to know and something you wish to do, and Life understands this. That is why you are reading this.

Here is what you wish to know . . .

*98% of the world's people
are spending 98% of their time
on things that don't matter.*

You have been part of that 98%. Now you are no longer. From this day forward you choose to spend your time on The Only Thing That Matters. The question is, *what is that?*

Here is what you wish to do . . .

*Find your answer
to that question.*

This requires a deep exploration of the Self. You are in the right place for such an important and remarkable undertaking. Trust that. If you weren't in the right place to find your answer, you would not be here. Do not think you have come to this book by chance.

Do not think that.

Think this: *My Soul knows exactly what it is doing.*

Also, think this: *My Soul already knows what really matters.*

So it is not a question of "finding" that answer, it is a question of *remembering.* It is not a process of discovery, it is a process of recovery. This data does not have to be *researched,* it merely has to be *retrieved.*

~

Let's begin here.

Something very unusual is occurring on this planet right now. You have no doubt noticed it. It may be producing a more than normal amount of challenge and disjointedness in your life, and perhaps even some major upheavals. You are probably noticing it in the lives of others as well.

For a while you may have thought that this was all just your mind playing tricks on you; that things were not really happening any differently, and that you're just a little tired, a little overcommitted, a little oversensitive.

But now, as each day presents itself with obstacles mounting and challenges increasing and more and more personal issues coming up to be faced and healed, it is apparent that all of this is not an illusion, not an exaggeration. So you may be asking: "Why is all this happening? What am I doing wrong?"

And here's the answer . . .

You're doing *nothing* wrong.

AND . . . there *is* something very unusual going on right now in your life, and all over this planet.

~

Call it an energy shift, call it a cosmic cycle, call it the overhaul of humanity, or whatever you will, but what's occurring on Earth right now is, you can be sure, very real. It's touching lives emotionally, physically, and spiritually. Some lives more than others, but none are immune.

This experience is global in scope. Talk to people. Just ask them. Talk to people anywhere, everywhere. They'll tell you: Yes, life has been tumultuous lately. More than usual. More than normal. For some, more than ever.

Now there's a danger here, and that danger is not in what is happening, but in how you may *construe* what is happening. The danger is that you will view what's going on as "bad," and then react from utter frustration or fear, or even anger (which is Fear Announced), doing exactly the opposite of what would serve you.

The biggest danger is that because of the inaccuracy of your perception, you will miss a once-in-a-lifetime (*literally* a once-in-a-lifetime) opportunity.

The good news is that your Soul is working hard to make sure you don't do that. It is working at this right now, *in this moment.*

One last time: Do you really think it is *happenstance* that you are reading this . . . ?

2

Can You Believe This?

LIFE LOVES YOU. It may not seem that way to you right now, and you may guffaw when you hear this, but Life loves you and is supporting you, and that is why *you are receiving a Special Invitation from Life on this day.*

You may actually be able to feel this invitation—much as you sometimes sense in the sleepy hours of the morning that it's time to wake up.

Have you ever had that feeling? Nothing in particular is happening. There's no alarm going off. No one has come into the room to stir you. There's just an inner knowing: *It's time to wake up.*

You may be feeling these days a muted excitement stirring within, generating a restless readiness to respond to a gentle but persistent inner voice that keeps whispering . . .

. . . IT DOESN'T HAVE TO BE THIS WAY.

~

That inner voice is correct. Your life does *not* have to be a series of worrisome and challenging crises involving finances or relationships or health or family—or all of the above. Or, for that matter, on some days nothing in particular . . . just a nagging sense of *out-of-orderness.*

Neither does the world at large have to be a container of constant calamity engulfing its governance and politics, its commerce and economics, its environment and ecology, its cultures and religions.

Listen to that voice . . .

. . . IT DOESN'T HAVE TO BE THIS WAY.

That is not wishful thinking. That is your Awareness speaking.

What is occurring in your life right now is that your Awareness is growing—and now you are hearing its voice.

In strictest terms a "growth" in your Awareness is not possible. Your Awareness is what it is; it does not "grow" larger and larger. That's because your Awareness rests within your Soul, and your Soul does not get bigger, or in some way "more," than it always was and is now.

It is your *Mind* that expands. For easy understanding, it could be said that Awareness rests in the Soul and Attention resides in the Mind.

So to put what is occurring in your life another way, you are now paying *greater Attention* to your Awareness. It's one thing to be "aware," but it is another thing altogether to pay attention to what your Soul is aware of (instead of ignoring it, which most people do most of the time).

This mixture of the two is what might be called Consciousness. When your Mind pays attention to your Soul, and your Mind and Soul thus carry the same data, hold the same idea, and possess the same perspective, you might be said to be *fully conscious.*

So, in real terms, it is your Consciousness that is expanding as the Awareness of your Soul comes to the Attention of your Mind.

Now here's where the danger of misinterpretation exists: Your increased Consciousness brings along with it *an increased sensitivity to every aspect of life*. This has no doubt resulted in an expansion of the *effect* that all of Life has on you—and this could feel as if everything's *in your way*, standing between you and peace, because the same kinds of life experiences that you encountered with little difficulty just a short while ago now feel like they're going to put you on "overload."

You've probably been wondering what's going on, and why you don't seem to be "handling things" as easily anymore.

Well, it's all very simple: You're not becoming less able, you're becoming more capable than ever. But you're *growing into that* as Life calls upon you to pay more attention to more things in more ways more of the time.

Add to this the fact that there is more data *in toto* of which you can *become* aware (the world's new technologies have placed more information at the fingertips of a 15-year-old today than that to which the President of the United States had access a few years ago)—and you can see the challenge.

And it hasn't stopped there. More things seem to be falling apart all at once all over the place than ever before—from financial systems to political systems to social systems, and even weather systems.

So here you are, in the middle of The Perfect Storm: a confluence of expanding energies, enlarging noticements, and rapidly multiplying negative events that are producing some very interesting times. To say the least . . . some

Very.

Interesting.

Times.

Yet it is as spiritual teacher Mary O'Malley wonderfully and succinctly puts it: "What's in the way *is* the way."

~

The reason that life's events seem to many people to be *in the way* is that many people have no idea *where they're going*. They do not know that on the path they were *intended* to take, there *are* no obstacles.

The obstacles that people are encountering have not been plunked down suddenly and ruthlessly by Life, right in the middle of the path they're traveling. Rather, the path they're traveling *is the one with obstacles already on it.*

Why? Why would people be traveling the road with all the detours, all the pitfalls and potholes and stumbling blocks, and finally, all the dead ends?

It's because they've been given poor directions, or a very badly drawn map.

The way people have been *told* they're supposed to go is not the way they *came* here to go. And *that* is why 98% of the world's people are spending 98% of their time on things that just don't matter.

When you turn *that* around, you'll turn your *life* around.

3

It's Important That You Know
That You *Know* What You Know

You already know this. At the deepest part of your being, you already know what has just been said. Your purpose in coming to these pages is not to find out something you don't know, but to remind yourself of what you *do* know—so you may *know* that you know.

"Knowing that you know" is a major step in living a life focused on The Only Thing That Matters. You may have *forgotten* that you know that you know, but the very first Remembrance brought to you here corrects all of that. The very first Remembrance is that you know that you know. Now you *remember* that you know that you know—because now you have "remembered that you remember."

There will be many other equally important Remembrances in the explorations just ahead. These Remembrances—what you might call "Soul Knowings"—are precisely what your Soul brought your Mind here to encounter. So you may want to keep track of them.

～

It is impossible to overstate the impact of "knowing that you know." Remembering that you *know* that you know releases you immediately from any thought of helplessness, hopelessness, and haplessness. Yet once

now, you will yearn to know *what* you know, *specifi-*
want to know what your *Soul* is aware of.

ul that your deepest awareness lies, for awareness
edge, and your Soul is where true knowledge is found.

perience—which is
edge.

ou may ask: "How
is Knowledge that I
?"

Very good question.

> *A Soul Knowing:*
> You already know
> all that you need to
> know, and you *know*
> that you know.

And the answer? The simplest way to
retrieve information that you already
hold about life (but may have forgotten that you hold—or forgotten how
to access) is to *call it forth.*

This is another way of saying: Bring it *forward*. Place it at the fore-
front of your thoughts.

You can do this in two ways.

One way is to gather it from a place that appears to be outside of you.
That is what you appear to be doing right now.

A second way is to gather information from a place that is *inside* of
you. That is what you are actually doing right now.

It *looks as if* you are doing the first, but you are actually doing the
second.

~

You are being invited to meet Yourself here—and that is precisely what
you came here to do. (To *Earth,* not just to this book. But it will *happen*
in this book, and be demonstrated in a most unusual way.)

One of the things that you already know, but that you sometimes
forget, is that *nothing happens by accident,* and that *there's no such thing as
coincidence.*

It is because you know this is true that the appearance of this book in
your life at this exact moment cannot exactly be a shock.

Of course, it wasn't intended to be a shock. It was intended to be a *confirmation*. And confirmation is very timely *on this exact day,* because there are energies, situations, and circumstances in your life right now that have tempted you to seriously *question* what you know—if not deny it altogether.

Don't do that.

Do.

Not.

Do.

That.

That will not serve you.

This will.

Moving even more fully into this moment and this experience will.

Trust that your Soul knows, always, what will next serve you. In fact, that is *why* what happens next *happens next.*

4

You're About to Become an Author

Now WAIT UNTIL YOU SEE what happens next. You're not going to believe what happens next.

You're going to be writing this book.

"That's crazy," you could say. "I'm *reading* this book, not *writing* it." Ah, yes, but wait. Magic is about to happen.

~

Have you ever heard the statement: *We are all One?* Of course you have. You've heard it a thousand times. But have you ever considered what it would be like if it were *true?* Not just conceptually, but actually, *factually, functionally?*

Well, it *is* true.

Actually.

Factually.

Functionally.

There's no one else except You, in various forms.

To many people this at first sounds "way out," and too abstract to embrace as a working notion of reality. Yet considered within a larger context, a very broad context, it might begin to fall within at least the outer reaches of the realm of possibility.

Let's take a look.

All of us are made of the "same stuff," having evolved from the same First Source. To use an analogy: When the ocean first appeared, and then expanded, it was not created as something other than its drops. A drop of the ocean is the same as the ocean. It *is* the ocean, in smaller form. No single drop is *other than* the ocean. All the drops of the ocean are One Thing: THE OCEAN.

It would not, therefore, be inaccurate for one drop of the ocean to say to another drop: "We Are All One." The second drop would simply say, "Of course we are. Just because we have been *singularized* does not mean we are *other than* each other, nor are we other than that of which we are a singularization. We are all the same thing, The Ocean, in singular form."

> *A Soul Knowing:*
> We are all the Same
> Thing, individuated.

This is also true about human beings. We are all the Same Thing, simply individuated. We are not separate from That From Which We Have Emerged, nor are we "other than" each other.

～

Now you might think, "Well, that's all very nice, that's a very nice model of the world, but there's no way to put that into practice in the reality of our daily lives."

And it would be understandable if you thought that. We are, after all, appearing to be separate beings, even if we aren't in fact. We are, to be sure, acting as if we are separate beings—even if we are all the Same Stuff. We are acting so much so that if the various Parts of Us told *other* Parts of Us that We think there is only One of Us, the other Parts of Us would laugh at Us.

And if We *insisted* that We Are All One, the other Parts of Us would do more than laugh at Us. They would put Us away somewhere, so that We could not contaminate the rest of Us. And if that didn't shut us up . . . well . . . they would have to take other measures.

Why? Why all this ominous stuff that sounds as if it's coming out of a bad movie? Because the idea that We Are All One *upsets every applecart in the world.*

It upsets our global economy for sure. How would we proceed?

It upsets our global polity for sure. How would we proceed?

It upsets our global society for sure. How would we proceed?

And . . . here it comes . . . watch out now . . . it upsets our global theology for *absolutely, positively* sure. How would we proceed?

Everything we thought was true would not be true. Everything we thought was *not* true would be true. How would we be able to stand up for ourselves? How would we be able to fight for what is right? How would we be able to justify *killing* each other over what is right if we thought that we were killing *ourselves* over what is not even true?

～

Okay, so maybe We should just drop the whole idea. Erase the statement: We Are All One.

Forget We said that.

Allow yourself to encounter this material as if someone else wrote it and you're just reading it. Maybe that's enough for the first sit-down with this book. That's the safe way, and so it may be the better way. At least for now. Perhaps We can get back to this a bit later . . . like, maybe, 10 chapters from now . . . after more groundwork has been laid.

Or maybe not. We'll see.

No, wait. We have to. It's an absolute Must, because it's this Awareness that creates the only context within which The Only Thing That Matters can emerge as an experience in our lives. So before we're done here, you're going to be invited into a felt sense that We Are All One—because *you're going to be writing this book.*

But not just yet.

～

For now, let's get back to the original literary style. That style assumes this book is being written by someone else and you're reading it. Let's accept that idea and return to the original question: What *does* matter? And . . . if you pay attention to only *that* . . . what of the *rest* of your life?

How do you live in this world without paying attention to the things that you used to spend 98% of your time on? Hang out in a cave? Enter a monastery? Become an ascetic? "Drop out," as thousands did in the sixties counterculture of hippies in communes disillusioned with conventional values?

No. The idea here is not to walk away, or to walk around in a meditative daze, abandoning all constructive activity. The idea is to *refocus* your life's intention, so that one day it may be said that 98% of your time is being spent on things that *do* matter.

The surprise here will be that when this happens, your activities themselves probably won't change very much. Even if everyone on the planet read this book, agreed with it, and began spending 98% of their time on what *does* matter, people's activities wouldn't change that much.

People would still get up and go to work—or create some way to survive.

People would still marry and have kids—or create someone to love and by whom to be loved.

> A *Soul Knowing:*
> It is not what you do, but how and why you do it, that makes it matter.

People would still run and jump and dance and sing and laugh—or create some way to entertain themselves, to bring joy into their days and nights, and to be happy.

So the question becomes: if what humans do won't change that much, what will make what they do suddenly *matter?*

The answer lies not in what they do, but in *how and why they do it.* The answer is: something matters if it leads to and produces a particular kind of result—a result desired by the Soul. A result desired by Life Itself.

It is when the way in which you are doing anything *facilitates* the Larger Goal that you are seeking to reach that it *matters.*

Yet what human beings are doing cannot facilitate what they are trying to accomplish if they don't *know* what they are trying to accomplish. They must be aware of the Larger Goal they are seeking to reach. And therein lies the problem. *Most people don't know what they're doing.*

That is not meant in any way pejoratively. It is a simple statement of fact. Most people have little understanding of the nature of the Journey they are on, much less how to arrive at their desired destination.

It is the things they are doing day-to-day that play a huge role in moving them toward, *or away from,* their Larger Goal, yet most are not aware of where they were intending to go to begin with, and so, as one comedian wryly noted: "If we're not careful, we'll all wind up exactly where we're headed."

Today the earth is populated with billions of people desperately hoping to "get somewhere," but having no idea of where they're going.

The first step in moving into clarity on where you're going is moving into clarity on where you are *right now,* on *who* you are to *begin* with, and on *why* you are *here.*

On Earth, that is.

What are you doing here? What is the point of this? What is Life's purpose?

These are the questions that have to be answered before you can begin to make decisions about The Only Thing That Matters—to say nothing of living your daily life focused on that. So the next few chapters—Part Two of this book—will be devoted to a deep investigation of these very questions.

As you move through these next pages, know that this is an exploration for which your Mind has earnestly yearned. Your Mind, you see, has been trying for years to make sense of a life that makes no sense at all. Now, thanks to the Knowledge of your Soul, you will be placing everything that is happening in your life into a new context—a context in which life finally *does* make sense.

(NOTE: If you're a bit impatient at this juncture and do not wish to engage in this investigation right now, but would rather move directly into a discussion of what it looks like to focus your life in such a way that 98% of what you do *does* matter, feel free skip ahead to Part Three of this book. But just to let you know: you're very likely to wind up going back to Part Two eventually, reading through the deep explorations in Chapters 5–18, because it is there that the whole construction of Life—which is what *makes* The Only Thing That Matters *matter*—is defined and described.)

Part Two

Explaining life's biggest
mysteries, and why there is
only one thing that matters.

Oh, yes . . . and also revealing
what that is.

5

Back to Basics

DEAR SWEET AND GENTLE BEING . . . As we move more deeply into
this exploration, let us step back and take a look at some fundamental
concepts, including this one: You are on a journey here. And no, it is not
the journey from birth to death. It is a journey from way before birth to
long after death.

The importance and the implication of this Journey upon which you
find yourself can barely be comprehended by your Mind. It can be comprehended . . . but barely.

Is this because your Mind is so incapable, so inefficient? No. It is because
your Mind has been given so little information about the Journey itself.

We learn about it in a very indirect way. Not because our elders and
our teachers sit us down and tell us everything we need to know about it
(they have, after all, been given no more information than they are giving
us), but because our art has done the best it can to fill the gap.

It is humanity's culture that tells us about the experience in which we
find ourselves. (And this is why, by the way, the movement to remove "cultural pursuits"—music and drama, art and other creative expressions—from
our schools, leaving classrooms full of children to look only at our history, is
so crushingly damaging to our sense of who we are and why we are.)

We need culture and esoterics—story and song, movies and plays,
fiction and poetry, and really good television—to tell us about ourselves
in fuller ways.

The American poet Em Claire did just this, capturing the essence of our journey, when she wrote . . .

I left The Home so long ago now
that I would not recognize my own face.
I constructed the Boat of my Life
and I set out
into the open sea
waving to all who knew
that the seas would give me
everything I could handle
and everything I could not
and yet they waved, and I set out
into the open sea
In the Boat of My Life:
built from Soul, crafted by Heart
and with great innocence I pushed off
into the open sea
and have been away from my Home
so long now that I would not recognize my own face
but I know that Home
Home
remembers me

.

———

"Long at Sea"
©2007 em claire

⌒

This feeling and sense of being "away from home" is common to many people who yearn for the knowing and the experiencing of their union with the Divine.

Yet are we in the fullest sense "away from home"?

No. We are neither away from home nor away from God, but it sure seems that way. The tiny amount of information that we have been given by those who simply write about our history and our physical sciences has been wholly lacking in any truly important metaphysical or spiritual detail. Or, worse yet, it has been riddled with error.

All of that is going to end here.

⌁

You've brought your Mind to this self-exploration to remember three things: (a) the purpose of your life's journey, (b) the paths that this journey can take, and (c) the journey's destination.

Your remembering will begin with some more basics. But first, a request—from your Soul to your Mind:

Because these *are* "basics," much of what you will read in these next few passages may feel like "old news" to you. Have patience, then.

A gentle request, yes?

It is not a bad thing to be reminded of what you already know. Most people are not *applying* what they already know anyway, and that's the point. Perhaps a memory jog would be really good right about now.

And perhaps there are one or two tiny pieces of data that are not fully remembered—the remembering of which could change everything.

So please, have patience.

Now then . . . to those basics.

⌁

You are not your body. Your body is something you have.

You are not your mind. Your mind is something you have.

You are not your soul. Your soul is something you have.

Who, then, are you?

You are the sum total of all of these things—a loving, caring, sensitive, compassionate sentient being that *has* these things—and each of these things has a purpose and a function that serves the agenda of all three.

This Body/Mind/Soul trio will be referred to in this self-exploration as The Totality of You.

The function of the Mind is to guarantee the survival of the current physicalization of The Totality of You for as long as it takes to fulfill the Soul's Agenda.

> *A Soul Knowing:*
> You are the sum total of the Body, Mind, and Soul, and each of these aspects of you has a purpose and a function, but only one has an agenda: the Soul.

The function of the Body is to gather data from the physical environment to assist the Mind in guaranteeing your survival, and to place within that environment, in physical form, the nonphysical ideas, concepts, and decisions of the Mind.

The function of the Soul is to experience as many aspects as possible of Who and What It Really Is, using the Body, the Mind, and the physical environment in which It has placed Itself, as tools with which to accomplish this.

~

Because your Mind has been given little—or worse yet, totally inaccurate—information about the Soul's Agenda (which is *Life's* agenda), neither your Mind nor your Body can very often serve that agenda well— unless it is working in *conjunction* with the Soul.

Right now, if your Mind does not know what the Soul knows, your life could feel as if it's being pulled in different directions. Indeed, your very purpose for being on Earth could wind up being compromised—if not completely ignored.

This is, in fact, the circumstance in which most of humanity finds itself today.

What must happen if you wish to live a life that serves its actual purpose is that your Mind must bring into its database that of which the Soul is already aware, so that you can produce the *experience* of it. The Soul holds Knowledge, while the Mind creates the Experience of what you call Reality.

This is the very reason that The Totality of You came into the physical realm: to Experience that of which It has full Knowledge. Yet if the Mind's data does not *include* the Soul's Awareness, the continuing experiences the Mind creates will not be expressions of what the Soul knows—and that will *not* serve The Totality of You.

It is very important to understand that the "database" from which you may construct any present reality (i.e., the information that is stored within you), exists in *two different places* and is accessed in *two different ways*.

The challenge in human life is that most people do not know this—or *do* know it, but have not yet learned how to shift their point of focus from one well of information to the other at will . . . much less bring the two together.

What is being said here is that data about Life is held in "memory" within the Totality of You—and that one kind of memory is Physical, while the other is Metaphysical. The first kind of memory we have called Experience and the second, Knowledge. The first type of memory produces Desire (a yearning for more experience), the second reveals Intention (a yearning for a particular *kind* of experience—based on Knowledge, not prior Experience).

As you may have guessed, the first kind of "memory" is held in the Mind, the second in the Soul. The Mind captures, categorizes, files, and brings forward memories of every experience your Body and Mind have ever had. The Soul is the repository of all Knowledge about Who You Are,

Where You Are, Why You Are Where You Are, and all other aspects of Everlasting Life. This Knowledge is what has also been called here your Awareness. The terms are used synonymously.

As explained earlier, the *sum* of these two "data banks" is what humans call Consciousness. You no doubt have often heard the term "consciousness raising." This refers to the increase or expansion of the Mind's database—its limited storehouse of Experience—to include more of the Soul's unlimited Knowledge or Awareness of Life.

Experience+Awareness=Consciousness.

> *A Soul Knowing:*
> When your Present Experience and your Present Awareness are joined together, the Mind's Desire and the Soul's Intention become One.

The level of your Consciousness depends upon how much Experience you have had not only of your physical life, but also of your metaphysical life, the knowledge of which exists in your Soul's Awareness.

When, in any particular moment, your Present Experience (that is, the experience you are now having, rather than your memories of previous experience) and your Present Awareness (that is, the awareness to which you now have given yourself access) are joined together, the Mind's Desire and the Soul's Intention become One.

This is, truly, a marriage made in heaven: the merging of the Mind and the Soul. And *what God hath joined together, let no man put asunder.*

6

Remembering Again

APOLOGIES IF THIS is starting to sound a bit like a college lecture in Metaphysiology, but the topics we've been exploring are things you'll want to know about if you wish to live your life focused on The Only Thing That Matters.

Here is one more example of information you'll find it good to have: It is impossible for the human Mind to hold at one time *all* of the Knowledge held by the Soul.

As marvelous and sophisticated as the Mind's circuitry is, those circuits would "fry" if they were exposed in one single instant to the sum of what the Soul knows. It would be like attempting to direct all the electricity serving your house to a single outlet. Or, to use a different analogy, like trying to absorb the ocean with a sponge.

Yet suppose that sponge was wrung out at least a bit every so often, releasing some of the water that it was holding? Then it *could* continue sopping up the ocean.

This is a simplistic allegory of how the Mind works. The Mind's capacity is finite. The Soul's source in infinite. The Mind's "sponge" can access the Soul's Knowledge, and can really "sop it up," but can retain only so much at one time. If there's too much input, the Mind must "ring itself out" to avoid being overloaded. Hence, the Mind "forgets" some of what it once "knew."

This is exactly what has been happening with you.

～

The process in which you are now engaged is a process of retrieving what the Mind has forgotten, or released, of what it knew. For this reason much of what you are now being told (what you are now "remembering") will seem like "stuff you've always known."

It will feel as if there's "little new" here—and yet, the "renewal" of your *remembering* will "bring to Mind" information that's good to have your hands around again, because it is going to prove very valuable at this point in your life. And that is another way your Mind works. It knows what information you *now need,* what data you require *in this moment,* and it can reach into its millions of memories (like the countless files on your computer that you forgot were even there) and retrieve it, calling it forward *exactly when you need it.*

> A Soul Knowing:
> The quality of your life is determined by what you pay attention to.

So your Mind brings forward what you need to know, and puts waaaay on the back shelf what you have no urgent need for. Or, to continue now with our computer analogy, while your Mind is adding data to the file currently open on its desktop, it is closing other files to make the operating system run smoother.

History is replete with stories of veritable geniuses (Einstein, Edison, Steiner, etc.) who couldn't find their own glasses. (The file labeled GLASSES: LOCATION has been closed.) They could find the keys to the Universe, but they couldn't find the keys to their own house.

Such a person is often called *absentminded*—and that is a perfect description. Certain data is *absent from their Mind* so that other data—data which they, themselves, judge to be far more important—can be accommodated there.

And so it is that the more you remember, the more you'll forget. How this shows up in your life, how it affects your day-to-day functioning, will depend on which data you choose to retain.

If you decide that the latest sports scores, or the plotline and character names of the latest hit movie, or the best strategies to help you win the newest video game, are more important than the whisperings of your Soul, then that is the data you will hold on to, and the wisdom of your Soul will barely be heard . . . much less retained.

You will determine the quality of your life by what you pay attention to.

~

It is precisely *because* the Mind's capacity is finite and the Soul's is infinite that, if the Mind wishes to review the data of the Soul, it will need to do so in bits and pieces. You sometimes call these bits and pieces "lives."

The Mind brings in the Soul's Knowledge one lifetime after another, gradually turning it into Experience, then storing this Knowledge as "memories" within the Mind—a Mind which travels with the Soul lifetime after lifetime.

(Surprised? Wait. All of that will be explained in just a bit.)

When a person's Mind retrieves data from a previous lifetime (an enormous amount of anecdotal evidence suggests that this is a common occurrence), that person is often called a "prodigy"—demonstrating skills and abilities, wisdom and insight far beyond what present life experience would seemingly render possible.

~

When, within a given lifetime, that blending of the Mind and Soul of which we have spoken occurs, the Journey on which you find yourself will finally begin to make more and more sense, because you are taking that Journey in a state of expanded Consciousness. Your perspective will have shifted, and greatly enlarged.

Until such a blending of Experience and Knowledge occurs, however, your life will very often (perhaps, most often) *not* make much sense. And if you are using the data of the Mind alone (which the majority of people do the majority of the time) you may do nothing but frustrate yourself trying to *get it* to make sense.

Then you will run from pillar to post, from book to book, from lecture to lecture, from sermon to sermon, from workshop to workshop, and from teacher to teacher seeking answers.

The good news is that you don't have to run yourself ragged like this anymore. You don't have to go anywhere or do anything. Everything you've ever needed is where you are, within you, right now. You've never really "needed" it at all, in the sense of not having it. You've simply needed to access it.

Yes, yes, we know . . . this is the Mantra of the New Age (and the teaching of Ancient Masters as well): "All that You Seek is Within You." And so it must be asked: If it is true, why is everyday life on a personal level the way it is? And why is the world in a constant state of crisis?

It is because—here we go again—98% of the world's people are spending 98% of their time on things that don't matter. They are ignoring the wisdom of their Soul, either because they are not aware of it (they are not "aware of their Awareness"), or because they do not know how to *access* what they are aware of when they need to. They "talk a good game," but they don't play it so well.

If either has been the case with you, it won't be much longer. If neither has been the case with you, you will very soon have remembered the articulations that can help others, for whom it *has been* the case.

Clearly, it is for these reasons that you have come here.

7

Moving Past "Oh No!"

By now you have already accessed several pieces of important data. Here is another: The Journey you are on, spoken of earlier, is a Sacred Journey, fulfilling a Divine Purpose.

Now the words "sacred" and "divine" can be a real push back, we all know. They can produce an immediate groan of "Oh no" from people who don't want to hear about either the "sacred" *or* the "divine." They present a special challenge to those who once embraced those terms with enthusiasm, but who have since moved away from organized religion and its dogmas.

Yet the journey and the purpose that will be described here bear no resemblance to the doctrines of Standard Brand Theology. Indeed, that theology would call it heresy.

Talk of a Sacred Journey and a Divine Purpose may also be challenging to people who have never believed in any kind of divine presence at all, to say nothing of a "divine purpose."

But now, some common ground: Everyone—atheists, agnostics, and antagonists alike—believes in Life, for that is humanity's common experience. And so the invitation here is to get past simple verbiage that can lead to "Oh *no*," and go straight to inner wisdom that can lead to "Oh *my.*"

"Life" is that which is larger than any individual or any particular belief system. It is that which animates all of existence. Its energy is found everywhere. Without its energy, nothing that is, is. All that ever was, is now, and ever will be arises out of Life.

Life is something that is obviously happening. It is expressing in, as, and all around every person. No one can deny Life's presence. The only challenge remaining, then, is one of semantics.

If we decide to call Life "God," the life journey becomes a Sacred Journey. It is simply a matter of what words one uses to describe a single phenomenon.

So if the word "God" stops you in your tracks, read the word "Life" wherever you see the word "God." It won't change a thing in the meaning. And if the word "Divine" pushes you back, substitute the words "Life Serving." And if the word "Sacred" brings discomfort, use the word "Important."

Thus we see that the Journey you are on is an Important Journey, fulfilling a Life Serving Purpose. What may not be very clear is precisely what that purpose *is*. Yet your own remembering has expanded to the point where you now see clearly that Life has an intelligence all its own. (The Universe does not need "instructions" on how to run; the tiniest cells of living matter know exactly what they need to do to replicate and survive.)

> *A Soul Knowing:*
> The journey you are on is a Sacred Journey, fulfilling a Divine Purpose.

You can see at a glance that Life is unspeakably magnificent in its design, that it is incomprehensibly sophisticated in its functioning, and that every event and outcome is a part of that design.

Your intuitive understanding also tells you that Life's very essence, its foundational energy, can be focused and directed by Life Itself with specific intent to produce specific outcomes—and that, since *you* are part of the basic intelligence that is Life Itself expressing, *you* can focus and direct *your* Life energy with specific intent to produce specific outcomes.

All of this understanding is the beginning of living in a way that matters. It is by no means the All of it, but it is the Start of it. You merely have to remember how to get *on* with it.

That is what you are doing here.

⟡

You have drawn yourself, in this very moment, to an *outward writing of your inward knowing.*

Do not be surprised, then, if your experience here is very much like reading your own diary, misplaced long ago, but now found. As you encounter each new paragraph you may have a sense of knowing already what you are seemingly being introduced to now.

It is your Soul that holds this Awareness—to which your Mind is now being reintroduced.

The word Soul, of course, is another one of those words that many people resist. Many people do not even believe that they *have* a Soul. Or if they believe they do, they have no idea what the Soul *is,* or what it *does.*

What is its function? What is its purpose? We know what the Mind does. We know what the Body does. *What does the Soul do?*

⟡

Some people may see the Soul as sort of a "conscience," or maybe as a kind of "guardian," or "angel" (or both)—standing off to the side, with a purpose that is probably good, but whose way of functioning is not at all clear.

Then there are those who *know* that they have a Soul, and who feel that the Soul has an agenda (in this they are correct), but who are so mixed up about what that agenda *is* that they are living lives that create more heartache and difficulty, self-deprivation and lack of joy than they were ever meant to (or need to) experience.

Still others—you among them—also know that the Soul exists, but are no longer willing to be trapped in Old Stories about the Soul's agenda.

You are ready to call into your Mind the Knowledge of your Soul regarding its True Agenda. There's an impulse deep within that makes you want to do this *now*. It comes from that part of you that looks at your life and whispers, *It doesn't have to be this way.*

It is, of course, your *Soul* itself doing the whispering, and leading the way on The Sacred Journey. Your Soul is not only *leading* the way, it is *showing* the way and *creating* the way.

It is not, however, *directing* the way.

Because the Soul is not the dictator here, demanding this and commanding that, your Body and your Mind may not always be going in the same direction as your Soul. And while this is the very essence of freedom, it can—as one might well imagine—create in one's life . . . how shall we put this . . . ?

Complications.

8

Surprising News about Your Body and Your Mind

LIFE'S BIGGEST COMPLICATIONS are those that present themselves when the Soul, the Mind, and the Body are all going in different directions. To understand how this can happen, it will help to know even more about The Totality of You.

The explanation here is going to get a little intricate or complex now, but once again you're urged to stick with it, because when this entire exploration is over, your whole life can change.

That is not an exaggeration. It is, in fact, a reasonable expectation.

~

Because the intricacy of the explorations here is recognized, the format of this presentation (as you surely have noticed) is to present its information in tidbits. By placing vast and complex information before the Mind in small pieces, the Mind can much more easily absorb it. This is not because the Mind is dull, it is because it sometimes simply needs a rest. So, if it serves you as you move forward, allow yourself to stop for a breather at any one of the many Pausing Junctures that have been inserted into the narrative text, indicated by this symbol . . .

~

When you come upon one of these natural stopping points, you may wish to do just that. Stop. Pause. Relax the Mind. Maybe silently consider what has just been read.

One wonderful tool is to actually *rewrite* what has just been read, in your own words, in a personal journal. The idea would be to put your thoughts about *these* thoughts in a place where you can access them easily, and that which will be much more personal to you than a book on a shelf that you may not pick up to read again for months.

People tend to read their personal journals much more frequently than they reread books—even good books that they got a lot out of. Somehow a journal entry, with the ideas found here expressed in your own words, will seem much more compelling to your Mind a year from today than this book itself.

Give it a try.

~

One more note about what's written here, please:

To promote easier absorbing and consideration of the many metaphysical abstractions this text contains, you will find in our continuing explorations here some circling back over broad concepts and some repetition of specific ideas. This redundancy is not by accident. (Nor is it by accident that you have found your way to these ideas.)

~

So now, here is another of those ideas. It's a big one, one that many people have never considered or may not have even thought to consider before.

Your Soul has embarked on its Sacred Journey in a *single identity* eternally, while your Body and your Mind are configured in their present identity only on this particular "leg," your current leg, of your eternal travels.

Some people have interpreted this to mean that the Soul lives forever, while the Body and the Mind die. Indeed, that is the standard interpretation of most of the world's traditional religions. Yet it is not accurate.

The Body and the Mind do not die, any more than the Soul dies.

~

That is correct. The Body and the Mind never die.

As noted, this may be surprising information to some people. In fact, that's probably an understatement. It is possibly the greatest unknown or unrevealed aspect of Life. Ironically, it may also be the most important.

Why? Why is this important? Because it places into a whole new context the matter of Who You Are and Why You Are Here—and it is critical to understand *that* if you are to begin to focus your life on The Only Thing That Matters.

The very *reason* that 98% of the world's people are spending 98% of their time on things that don't matter is that they have misunderstood Who They Are or Why They Are Here—and they have misunderstood *that* because they have imagined that the Body and the Mind die, while the Soul lives forever.

As soon as we understand that we are three-part beings, and

> *A Soul Knowing:*
> The Body and the Mind
> do not die, any more
> than the Soul dies.

that the Body and the Mind *never* die, everything in how we look at life changes. So let us now examine the intricate nature and relationship of the Body, Mind, and Soul.

~

Now as we begin presenting these kinds of new ideas and embark on this portion of our exploration in earnest, please know there's a possibility that somewhere along the way you could be tempted to say: "This is all very interesting, but what does it have to *do* with anything? What does all this *esoteric stuff* have to be with my on-the-ground, 9-to-5 experience?"

You'll have a chance to say those things later! Right now you're going to be invited yet one more time to exercise patience, because you can't decide what really matters to you until you know and understand who this "you" that's being talked about here *is*—a point that will be made over and over on these pages. So here's a very short "primer" on the true nature of "you."

~

Everything in life is physical—including your Soul. What you think of as "nonphysical" is what you loosely think of as "invisible." Yet *visible* and *physical* are not the same thing, and many things that are invisible are physical, as you know.

Most people who believe in the existence of the Soul at all agree that the Soul lives forever. (Whether it spends eternity in "Heaven" or in "Hell" is a matter of differing theological persuasion, but there seems to be little argument among major religions that the Soul exists eternally.)

What most people have never been told is that the essential energy of which your Body and Mind are composed *also* never ceases to exist—although, unlike your Soul, they change form.

Your Body and your Mind could thus be called "shape-shifters." They can and do change shape or form throughout eternity. They do this *at the behest of the Soul,* which uses the Essential Energy that forms the Body and the Mind as its tools.

Think of a man who hammers out a new shape from white-hot steel, which is malleable and can be poured until it cools and hardens. The energy that forms the Body and the Mind is likewise "malleable" when it is "white hot"—or, in the language of metaphysics, when it shines brightly with the Light that Essential Energy emits in its essential state.

~

The shape of the Body and the Mind are altered when the oscillation of their energy vibration changes frequency—which it does when their energy moves into the Physical Realm. Certain frequencies of this energy vibration can make all or part of the Body invisible to humans. The Mind (not to be confused with the brain, which is part of the Body) is an example. It is invisible, but not undetectable. It is the energy package that animates the brain.

Yet while neither the Mind nor the Body are seen following what is called "death" (the Body usually having been buried or cremated, the Mind having simply "disappeared"), this does not mean they do not exist.

The Body certainly exists, you might reason, either in a slowly changing form, as a deteriorating corpse, or in the form of ashes that are more quickly absorbed by the rest of the physical world.

We think that this is the whole of the Body—all there is left of what once was. We say that the Body has been reduced to this. Yet it turns out that this is only the *residue*. In reality, a person's "remains" are literally and simply that: what "remains" in visible form. This is the least of the energy components that comprised your physical being. It is merely the part of your physical energy that continues to vibrate within a frequency range that allows the energy to be visible.

The largest portion of your physical energy shifts its vibration at the moment that you call "death," rendering it invisible to the naked eye.

～

Even now, before death, there are parts of you that are invisible. There are some humans who are reportedly able to view what are popularly called "auras," which they describe as energy fields that surround the Body. They actually are part *of* the body—and are but one example of the Body having parts that are not usually visible.

At death, your Body and your Mind immediately begin to transmogrify.

To understand this process a little more fully, consider a burning log in your fireplace. Most of the energy that *was* the log becomes invisible as it is released. It turns into at least three new energy forms that can be easily identified: light, heat, and smoke. Following this transmogrification, a residue remains. We call this residue the ashes.

It is clear to all that the ashes are but 5% of what was once a much larger physical object. *What happened to the rest of the log?* Can it be said that its energy is "dead"? No. *No energy ever dies.* Energy simply changes form. The rest of the log "went up in smoke." Or became the heat and light of the fire.

~

Your own Body and your Mind transmogrify in the same way. As the largest portion of the Essential Energy that was your Body and your Mind changes form, continuing to exist as part of The Totality of You, the tiniest portion of residue remains.

> *A Soul Knowing:*
> No energy ever dies. Energy simply changes form.

This is the portion of The Totality of You that you have chosen to leave behind. It continues to exist also, but *not inter-dimensionally.* You no longer wish to carry it with you. You're done with it. You're finished with that aspect of your Self. So you leave it in this particular dimension of Always/Everywhere.

What goes with you is what serves the Soul. This aspect of your Body and Mind later reconstructs itself at the instruction of the Soul. It may reconstruct itself in the present expression and dimension, returning You to this Life to live over again in a new way, or it may reconstruct itself in another expression and dimension, to live a "different" life as a different person, becoming what you call "reincarnated."

Throughout all of this the Soul's identity has not been, and never will be, changed. Only the Essential Energy of the Body and the Mind has been reassembled, in a new version of Life Expression.

9

Of Snowflakes and Trees

IT IS DIFFICULT FOR SOME PEOPLE to get their Mind around what you have just remembered. This is surely why Jesus and so many other masters chose to share some eternal mysteries through parables and stories. We are going to do the same thing here.

Again, this is not because the human Mind is so weak or underdeveloped. It is because the Mind has been given so much misinformation that there is virtually no *room* for vast, new, additional content until something has been deleted.

What you are now being invited to do is delete much of your Old Story about Life and how it is, Death and what it is, and God and who it is to make room for a New Story.

Here is a parable to help in the conceiving of that New Story . . .

The Parable of the Snowflake

Once upon a time there was a snowflake. It's name was Sara. Sara the Snowflake had a brother named Sam. Sam the Snowflake.

Sara and Sam both lived a good life—but they feared for the day that they would die, melting away into the nothingness. Then one day the Snow Angel appeared to both of them. "A snowflake is eternal. Did you know that?" the Angel said, and then the Angel explained:

"The very first snowflakes in the history of the world are the snow-flakes that are falling today. They fall from the sky as highly individual-ized physicalizations. There are no two snowflakes alike. There never have been, in all the history of snowflakes.

"The flakes are awesomely beautiful in their individual design. No one who watches them falling from the heavens can fail to see their exqui-site splendor. People run outside when snowflakes fall, beholding their breathtaking magnificence.

"As they land, they merge with one another. People call a huge collec-tion of them on the ground simply 'snow.' They don't say, 'Look at that big pile of snowflakes.' They say, 'Look at that mountain of snow.' They see all the individual snowflakes as One. And indeed, the snowflakes *are* One with One Another."

The Angel went on . . .

"Soon the sun comes out and the snow melts, each flake disappearing, one by one. They don't, of course, disappear at all. They simply change form. Now they are water, rippling together in a sparkling puddle or flow-ing together in a little stream.

"The sun continues to work its magic, and soon the water itself disap-pears. Or *seems* to. Actually, it, too, simply changes form. It evaporates, rising into the air as invisible vapors and gathering there in such concen-tration that they are visible again—as clouds.

"As more and more vapors gather, the clouds become heavy with their moisture. Soon, once again, the moisture falls, raining down upon the earth. And if the temperature is just right, the falling rain turns into snow-flakes again—no two snowflakes alike. Ever. In the history of snowflakes."

Sara and Sam were never so happy in their entire lives. Suddenly, everything was what you might call . . . *crystal clear.*

And so, in the snow we see the Cycle of Life and the Story of You.

~

There was never a time when You were not. There will never *be* a time when You will not Be. You appear from the heavens, physicalized as individual aspects of All That Is. While each physicalization is absolutely and gloriously non-identical, they are nevertheless All The Same Thing. And so they merge into a single essence, a particular life expression that you call "humans."

Then, to the heavens each Essence returns, once more *invisible-ized.*

You are not "no longer here," You are simply "no longer visible." Yet You exist, fully self-conscious and fully self-aware, until You return again to total visibility through full physicalization.

And here is a great secret. You are never *not* "physical." You are sometimes simply *less* physical. Even as a snowflake is never not physical. When it is snow, it is physical. When it is water, it is physical. When it is steam, it is physical. When it is vapor, it is physical. When it is moisture, it is physical. When it is unseen and utterly invisible, it is physical. When it falls from the clouds as rain, it is physical. And when it hits the freezing temperature beneath the sunlit clouds, it crystallizes, becoming a snowflake once again.

What a journey the snowflake has taken! Changing form, changing form, evermore changing form, finally returning as another snowflake, magnificently different from its earlier version, but still, in essence, the same.

And what a journey *you have taken.* It is a Sacred Journey, with a Divine Purpose.

～

The fact that the Body and the Mind remain with the Soul is evidenced in the testimony (and those testimonies now number in the thousands) of people who have had what are called NDE's, or Near Death Experiences.

These people often report that their Mind was fully aware of everything that was going on when they "crossed over" to the "other side." In some cases they even tell of experiencing themselves in their own Body, in its highest state of good health. But the Body isn't "heavy," as a snowflake falling to earth. It is light as vapor, as a snowflake not yet crystalized.

Many also report seeing and being greeted by loved ones who have "gone before"—and that these loved ones, too, appeared in *their* own bodies at the height of their health, each body as light as vapor.

What is being said here is that all expressions of physical life have the ability to transmogrify, and all life on earth *does so.*

Impossible! you say . . . but is it?

> "It's no use," cried Alice, "one can't believe impossible things!"
> "I dare say, you haven't had enough practice," replied the White Queen.
> "I always did it for half-an-hour a day. Why, sometimes I've believed
> six impossible things before breakfast."
>
> *Through the Looking-Glass* (Chapter 5)
> Lewis Carroll

Still, it is hard to imagine that Life goes on forever. As in, forever and ever, and even forevermore. The Mind searches for ways to comprehend it, given that there are no examples around us. Or are there . . . ?

The Truth of Trees

If you could sit at your window for many, many years and just watch the tree outside your house, you would see that the tree never dies, but simply changes form.

You might say, "Yes, but it began somewhere. It began with a seed." Yet where did the seed come from? "From another tree," you might say. But what if the truth is, *it's the same tree?*

Imagine a tree growing from a seed. The tree grows and grows and grows until one day, perhaps hundreds of years on, it stops growing and does the thing that you call "die." Yet it has not died. It has simply undergone a *process,* which includes creating seeds, which in turn have sprouted new trees. But are these really *new* trees . . . or merely the *same old tree starting over?*

When a tree reaches the grandest height that it is going to reach in its present form, it drops *itself* onto the ground. (That is, it ultimately falls over.) Yet the seed that it earlier dropped is not something else. It is *part of the tree*, just as a drop of ocean water is part of the ocean itself. We are simply giving *different names* to the *same thing in different forms.*

When the tree drops a seed, it is dropping *itself* onto the ground; it then plants itself *into* the ground, then experiences itself growing all over again, in what *appears to be another "body."* Yet it is the *same* body, having gotten smaller, and then bigger; having transmogrified.

You can even cause a tree or a plant to do this in *mid-cycle,* by taking a mere *clipping* from the tree and putting it into water, where it will sprout new roots, allowing it to then be planted into the ground.

Now, is this *another tree?* Or, miracle of miracles, is it the *same* tree, a part of which has been snipped off and replanted? *Where does one tree end and the other tree begin?* Because they are physically separated, does that mean they are not the *exact same Essence?*

In our limited human understanding, we have equated physical separation with essential differentiation. But what if there are no differences at the level of Essence?

There are not. And this is what is meant by Eternal Life.

It has been built into *every form of Life that exists.* From stars and planets to entire solar systems. Yea, to entire *universes.* From people and snowflakes and trees to entire ecosystems, and everything *in* them, each aspect of Life experiences the fact of its own eternal existence and its own Energy Essence in accordance with its own level of Consciousness.

What is this *Essence* that transfers from one snowflake to the next, from one tree to the next, from one solar system to the next, from one "physicalization" to the next, from one "lifetime" to the next?

It is The Only Thing There Is, *continually transmogrifying.* It is Divinity, indivisible but made individually visible, over and over again, through the expression that we call Life Itself.

It is the Single Soul, *reborn.* It is the One Thing, *multiplied.* It is God, *reshaped.*

It Was In The Beginning, Is Now, and Ever Shall Be, world without end. It is You.

10

There's Even More to Remember

OKAY, NOW IT'S FAIR to say it: "That's all very poetic, and this *has* all been very informative, but what *does* it have to do with me, with my life and my miseries and my challenges and my difficulties and, for that matter, even my joys? Can this now be related to my life, please? Because if it can't, I'm through with this discussion. I want to find out what *life* is all about; I want to hear about The Only Thing That Matters. I didn't come here to learn the fine points of universal cosmology."

Impatience at this point is fair. It would be very normal for you to react this way. The human Mind has been doing that—pulling people away from what they might most benefit from hearing—for a long time. We see, then, that what seems "fair" may not always be beneficial.

A case is being made here that your Soul and The Fundamental Essence of Life Itself are *the same thing, reshaped.* That is, you and all other things are One Thing, differing in form and composition, but identical at the level of Essence.

The information you have just received may not *seem* to have any practical application right now, but wait. The best part of this exploration has just begun.

~

There is something more that you have come here to remember than simply that the "traveling companions" moving through time are called Body,

Mind, and Soul and make up The Totality of You, or that the Soul goes on forever in the same form, while the Body and the Mind change form along the way.

The fact that your Body and your Mind *as well as* your Soul exist forever creates a whole new context for the living of your life, affecting dramatically the *how* and the *why* of it—for this fact suggests that your Body, Mind, and Soul are *equal parts of you* and are *meant to be used together.* This is not the way they are always used. In fact, for most human beings, this is not the way they are usually used, or even sometimes used. The number of people who operate from the Body, Mind, and Soul simultaneously is, relative to the total population of the earth, rather small.

And this is chiefly because the average person has not considered the Body and the Mind as part of a triumvirate. At least, not functionally. Perhaps conceptually, but not functionally. Yet they are aspects of the Triune that is The Totality of You, and *knowing* this allows you to understand that while your Soul is, in fact, "leading the way" on The Sacred Journey by clearing a path, your Body and your Mind, as equal free agents, are no less important on the eternal trek you are taking.

And because they are equal free agents, they *do not necessarily have to follow the Soul on its path.* And *that* piece of information is not inconsequential.

~

Even as parables and storytelling were used in the previous chapter, now let us employ the device of metaphor.

The dictionary defines METAPHOR as "a thing regarded as representative or symbolic of something else, esp. something abstract."

Well, there are few things more abstract than The Sacred Journey, so metaphor may be a useful tool here.

The Life Path Metaphor

In this symbolic story of how things are, your Body, your Mind, and your Soul are proceeding along a path. It is The Path of the Soul, called that not because your Soul is the only one taking it, but because your Soul is leading the way.

Yet while the Soul is leading the way, it is not requiring or demanding that its companions follow its lead. So, your Body and your Mind sometimes veer from The Path, setting out into the woods on either side, seeking a different adventure.

Tromping through the woods can seem like fun for a while if you imagine that you are only your Body and your Mind, but sooner or later you realize that you're much more than that . . . and then you begin to sense that you're taking a very long time getting to where the Much-More-Than-That seeks to go.

The American poet Robert Frost captured this feeling wonderfully when he wrote in a stanza of one of his most famous works . . .

> *The woods are lovely, dark and deep.*
> *But I have promises to keep,*
> *And miles to go before I sleep,*
> *And miles to go before I sleep.*

"Stopping by Woods on a Snowy Evening"
Robert Frost

~

The promises you have made have been entered into between you and yourself. They are promises to make more of this life than it seems to be; to be more *in* this life than you appear to be; and to give more *to* this life than you receive—so that Life Itself may be extended, with Its expression expanded. For it is the function of Life to create more Life through the Process of Life Itself.

Your promises, as part of all this, were not made at the level of Mind. They were entered into at the level of Soul, prior to your birth. And, of course, the word "promises" is a human term, used simply to get across an idea. A more accurate word might be "processes." These are the processes that Life Itself uses to ensure that Life Itself continues. These processes are encoded into your physical being as part of your very DNA—what might be called your Divine Natural Awareness.

~

When humans forget or ignore the fundamental processes of Life Itself they are, essentially, stepping off The Path of the Soul—which is the shortest path to where all humans yearn to go. The irony here is that at the same time they are leaving the Soul's path, humans complain that they are *not getting anywhere.*

This is the practical implication of the free agency of the Body and the Mind—what some religions call Free Will. And now you know why all of this has been examined here in such detail. This is about much more than the *esoterics* of universal cosmology. This has *on-the-ground implications* in everyday life.

> *A Soul Knowing:*
> Going the *long* way is not the same as going the *wrong* way.

The good news is that while it may appear that you are *not* "getting anywhere" when viewed from the perspective of Body and Mind alone, this is not true. You *are* getting somewhere, but because you have "strayed from The Path" and wandered into the woods, you are now getting to where you are going *the long way.*

Yet going the *long* way is not the same as going the *wrong* way.

This is very, very important for every human being to remember. Through this Awareness, hope can replace despair, and that is wonderful because while despair is blind, *hope has eyes.*

Now you can see that *others* have strayed from The Path and found themselves deep in the woods, just as you. Yet those who have gone before have tamped down the underbrush and inadvertently bent some of the branches in their rush to return to the Easier Trail, showing you, if you look closely enough, *the way back to The Path.*

So it may seem as if you are lost, yet you can find your way again if you keep moving forward, but start paying attention to the signs along the way.

The challenge, of course, is to notice them.

This is one of them. Are you noticing it? Are you paying attention to what your Awareness is showing you here?

11

The Most Important Question of Your Life

DEAR ONE . . . please understand that what you have just heard is not just word play. It is a statement, in the language of metaphor, of the human condition as experienced by many, many people. Perhaps, most people.

Some people have referred to the experience of taking the long way to where they wish to go as feeling "lost" or "without direction," and this can happen at any time during one's Sacred Journey, early or late . . . and more than once.

Now let's add to the metaphor here, so that through some further imagery you might get an even clearer picture of just what is going on.

The Life Path Metaphor – Part II

Think of the journey you are taking as a hike not only through woods, but woods that cover mountainous terrain.

While this hike is uphill and is challenging, there is that clear path that can make the challenge exhilarating and enjoyable.

Not all "challenge" has to be a negative or arduous experience. Certain challenges in life can be exciting and wonderfully rewarding. Yet a journey that is painful or arduous is what you may encounter if you stray too far from The Path and try to make your way to the top of the mountain through the thick forest.

What you could really use now is a Sherpa.

Enter: The Soul.

On this hike your Soul is leading the way for good reason. It has already been to the mountaintop, so *it knows how to get back*—and its way is the fastest way.

In fact, your Soul is at the mountaintop now.

That's right. The Soul is not really "going" anywhere. It already *is* where the Body and the Mind seek to go. The Soul, like God, is—already and always—Whole, Complete, and Perfect. It requires and needs nothing. It simply chooses to know itself in its own experience. In this, it is exactly like God. In fact, it *is* God, individualized.

The Totality of You—that is, your Body, Mind, and Soul *combined*—is thus both the journeyer and the destination. Part of It is journeying, and part of It is already where It is going. The purpose of the Journey is for the Totality of You to be able to experience what the part of you called your Soul already knows of you.

> *A Soul Knowing:*
> There is more than one way to the mountaintop, and there is no right way to get there.

By dividing your Self into three parts, you can both *know and experience at the same time* your true identity over and over again—your Body and your Mind assuming different forms from lifetime to lifetime, even as your Soul retains eternally its original and only form.

The purpose of the Body and the Mind taking different forms is to provide the Soul with endless *differing* expressions through which it can experience cyclical reunification with God, even as the Body and the Mind experience repeated reunifications with the Soul.

What the Soul is doing at the macro level, the Body and the Mind are doing at the micro level. It is all the Same Journey, taken by every Life Form, each in its own way, across the cosmos.

On your journey, the Soul is technically not *leading* you to your destination; it is *calling* you there. The Soul is going to keep showing the way and, by cutting through the thicket *from the other end* as it connects with your Mind and Body, creating the way. But, as mentioned, it will never *insist* that you *take* the way.

This is because your Soul knows that there is *more than one way to the mountaintop*, and that there is no "right way" to get there. There may be some ways that are *faster* than others, but "faster" doesn't mean "right." It simply means "faster."

⌒

"Faster" also does not necessarily mean less challenging. It does mean more direct, with more meaningful progress in each step, and therefore less time and energy expended.

And, of course, the term "faster" is used here within the context of Earth time, meaning the number of months or years of being human that it takes for The Sacred Journey of any particular individual to reach Completion.

And *Completion*, Dear Friend, is what the Journey is all about.

⌒

Completion is the goal.

It is the plan.

It is the aspiration, the wish, and the desire.

It is the target, the aim, the intention, and the ambition.

It is the brass ring. It is the Holy Grail.

What needs to be made clear now is how to *reach* Completion. What does that "looks like?"

If the Agenda of the Soul is to reach Completion on its Sacred Journey (and it is), there is only one question in Life that is truly important:

How does what I am doing right now serve the agenda of my Soul?

12

A Complete Explanation of "Completion"

THAT'S IT, THEN. Completion of The Sacred Journey is the Soul's Agenda. It is only through the experience of the Body, Mind, and Soul reaching Completion of The Sacred Journey that The Totality of You can fulfill The Divine Purpose.

We have not spoken of that Purpose yet (we will do so, extensively, in Chapter 14). Nor have we spoken of The Only Thing That Matters.

One thing at a time.

Yet this much please know: The Agenda of the Soul, The Sacred Journey, and The Divine Purpose are all facets of the same diamond.

～

The Mind and the Body daily cry out in bewilderment: *There is so much to see! There is so much to do! There is so much to be pleasured by, to be afraid of, to get excited about, to worry over, to be concerned with, to spend time on! What should I be focusing on? What should I be paying attention to?*

It is the Soul that daily answers the cry of the Body and Mind by telling The Totality of You what to focus on and pay attention to.

The Body and the Mind, however, are not always convinced that this is "the way to go." For one thing, traveling The Path does not always seem to the Mind and Body to be as much fun, and not nearly as much of an adventure as tromping through the unchartered territory of the woods on a snowy evening. Compared to this, The Path may seem boring.

Yet because the Journey has been described as "sacred" does not mean that one cannot seek and find pleasure and excitement in worldly pursuits. It does not mean that one cannot enjoy the thrills of life or grab all the joy that one can experience on a human level.

In fact, just the opposite is true. Because there will be less and less for you to be worried about—and eventually, nothing at all for you to be afraid of—you will at last be able to live your life to the fullest.

Yet what *is* living life "to the fullest"? What does a full life look like? A life filled with achievement? With fame? With fortune? With the love of one's family? With children raised wonderfully and sent off on a joyful path? With many things done and experienced? Just what, exactly, *is* a "full life"?

It is a life that brings the greatest satisfaction, which transcends all of these things. It is a life that follows the Path of the Soul.

~

As you follow the Path of the Soul you will find yourself doing many, if not all, of the things that you may have done if you had "strayed" from that path—but you will do them *for a different reason*, and thus, in a brand new way: a way that produces the Body and Mind's full physical expression of the Soul's metaphysical Essence.

> *A Soul Knowing:*
> When Essence
> becomes Expression,
> and Expression
> becomes Experience,
> The Totality of You
> has known Divinity.

When Metaphysical Essence becomes Physical Expression, Experience and Awareness become One, and The Totality of You has achieved Completion. And when The Totality of You achieves Completion, you behold the greatest joy you could ever imagine: the bliss of knowing Divinity, flowing through you, as you.

Now, here is an important piece of information: *This process is not a one-time thing.* It can happen many times during a single physical life. It can, in fact, happen many times during a single *day.* Indeed, it is the Soul's Agenda to create the perfect conditions for it to happen in *every moment,* and to make every moment a Holy Experience. And *that* is a "full life!"

(See *The Holy Experience,* a book describing the encountering of Life in this particular way. The book is free for the downloading at *www.cwgportal.com.*)

～

You may have already known that the Agenda of the Soul is something to which you should be paying attention, but it might not have been made clear to you just how important it is to your personal, earthly well-being.

Yes, not just to your spiritual well-being, but to your physical, psychological, emotional, social, and even financial well-being as well.

There is nothing else in Life that can bring you security, health, prosperity, happiness, and inner peace faster or more abundantly than the achieving of Completion. This is, of course, the opposite of what you have been told. There are, you have been advised, many other things to which you must pay attention.

You have been told that to be happy in Life you need to get the guy, get the girl, get the car, get the job, get the house, get the spouse, get the kids, get the better job, get the better house, get the promotion, get the grandkids, get the gray hair, get the office in the corner, get the retirement watch, get the illness, get the burial plot, and then get out.

You have been told that you need to obey God's commands, do God's will, follow God's law, spread God's word, and fear God's wrath, for when you face God's judgment you will be begging for God's mercy—and, depending on your offenses, you may not get it, but rather, may find yourself condemned to everlasting and unbearable torture in the fires of hell.

You have been told about the Survival of the Fittest and that To the Victor Go the Spoils, that Nice Guys Finish Last and that The One with the Most Toys Wins, that It's Every Man for Himself and that The End Justifies the Means, that Money Doesn't Grow on Trees and that You're to Be Seen and Not Heard and that You Are Not to Color Outside the Lines and that You Made Your Bed and Now You Have to Lie in It.

You have been told that There Is Only One Way to Heaven and You'd Better Get It Right, that It's Us Against Them, and that You Can't Fight City Hall; that you should Never Raise Your Head Above the Crowd, that You Can't Have Your Cake and Eat It, and that you should Never Count Your Chickens Before They Hatch.

Your Mind has been filled with many, many others messages that have created a day-to-day reality so far removed from your real reason for being on the Earth that it is a wonder you find any joy or excitement in life at all.

~

Now you are being told that the *only* thing that matters doesn't have to do with any of this. The missing puzzle piece revolves around how you reach Completion on The Sacred Journey of the Soul. Can this be true?

It can, and it is.

But don't worry; going where your Soul seeks to go will not deny you the Good Life. Completion of the Agenda of the Soul will get you everything that your Body and your Mind signal to you that they desire to enjoy. This is not about giving up one aspect of Life for another.

Trust that. Pay attention to the Soul's Agenda, and to what it takes to complete it, and the rest of Life—not only what you desire, but all that you may imagine that you need—will take care of itself. It will take care of itself *by* itself.

Or, to paraphrase a far more eloquent statement:

Don't go around asking,
"What are we to eat?" "What are we to drink?"
"Wherewithal shall we clothe ourselves?"
Seek ye first the Kingdom of Heaven,
and all else shall be added unto you.

The "Kingdom of Heaven" and "Completion of The Sacred Journey" refer to the same experience. The problem with both phrases is that no one has lately (if ever) explained or described to you what this experience *is,* and how to achieve it.

~

The Kingdom of Heaven is not a physical location, it is a State of Being. It is, in fact, the state of being "Complete." And so it is perfect that the two phrases are used here interchangeably.

It is literally "heaven" for humans to find themselves in a state in which there is nothing left to be, do, or have in any given Moment in order to experience inner peace, total love, and absolute bliss, because All That Is and all that one could ever desire is fully present, fully expressed, and fully experienced Right Here, Right Now.

You are Complete.

The Agenda of the Soul is to bring The Totality of You to this very State, so that the aspect of Life that is called "you" may express, experience, reflect, demonstrate, and *personify* the aspect of Life that is called Divinity.

This is your Basic Instinct.

~

Survival is the Basic Instinct of most chemical or biological life forms. It is what makes flowers turn toward the sun. It is what makes birds fly to warmer climates. It is what makes turtles recede into their shells. It is what makes lions roar and rattlesnakes shake their rattle.

Survival is not, however, the Basic Instinct of human beings—nor of any sentient creatures in the cosmos who have evolved into Self Consciousness. For such beings, the Basic Instinct is Divinity.

If your Basic Instinct were survival, you would run *away* from the flames of the burning house. But you run into the flames, because you've heard a baby cry. In that Moment *your survival is not the issue.*

> *A Soul Knowing:*
> The Kingdom of
> Heaven is not a
> physical location, it is
> a State of Being.

If your Basic Instinct were survival, you would turn away from the man with the gun. But you stand between the man and the person he is assaulting. In that Moment *your survival is not the issue.*

Something deep inside of you, something you cannot describe or name, calls to you in such Moments to demonstrate at the highest level Who You Really Are.

People who have done this, when interviewed by the newspapers later, never put it that way, of course. They say they simply acted on *instinct.* But it surely could not have been *survival* instinct, for their actions *defied* survival. Yet they had no fear—not even a *thought* of fear—at the time, because Who They Really Are *knows* that survival is not the issue. It *knows* that their survival is guaranteed. There are no questions about whether they will survive, the only questions are: How? In what form? Why? And for what purpose?

These become, in moments of self-realization, Life's Only Inquiries. And in moments of self-realization, the Mind and the Soul answer as One.

Instantly.

~

As a human, your Basic Instinct is on display when the Complete Being that is you is Completely Remembered, Recreated, Reintegrated, and Reunited with Divinity.

Even as the tiniest cell within you is a member of your Body, so is every element of physical Life a member of the Body of God. When the Mind's Experience and the Soul's Knowledge combine to produce elevated Consciousness, human beings choose to experience themselves once again as members of the Body of God. They are thus said to have Re-Membered.

This is what is meant by Completion.

13

Evolution Never Stops

THE EXPERIENCE OF COMPLETION is sheer ecstasy for The Totality of You because it is a reuniting and a reunion of *your* spirit with *The* Spirit (capital *T,* capital *S*).

It is a Holy Re-Membering. It is a coming home.

Recalling the words of Em Claire . . .

> . . . with great innocence I pushed off
> into the open sea
> and have been away from my Home
> so long now that I would not recognize my own face
> but I know that Home
> *Home*
> remembers me.

～

This holy Awareness can occur in any moment, and in many moments, during a person's life.

It is the nature of The Sacred Journey that makes this possible, for that journey is cyclical, undertaken and completed over and over again at ever-expanding levels of manifestation. It is very much like going through school, finishing one grade at a time.

When you are in third grade, you encounter again what you were introduced to in first and second grade, and you *now have an opportunity to apply it*. You also encounter what you had not encountered before: new and greater challenges, an opportunity to master more.

While perhaps useful, this is an imperfect analogy, because Life is not a school (although many spiritual teachers have told you that it is), and *there is nothing you need to learn*.

~

Like the tree outside your window, whose seed carried within it all the coding required for it to grow into what it has become, you arrived here knowing everything you needed to know to be everything you were designed to be.

As part of your encoding you have been given a higher level of Consciousness than the tree, of course, but you are in some ways not unlike like the tree, in that you are growing in stages. And like the rings of a tree, each phase of your life represents a specific period of your growth.

A Soul Knowing:
There is nothing you
need to learn.

Even as a tree has many rings, you conclude a Growth Phase and begin a New Growth Phase hundreds of times during a single life—and, indeed, *you have done this.*

And, at every time of Completion, a newly expanded agenda has been established. This is done *for* you, *by* you.

This is what you are doing right now.

What else do you imagine is going on here?

~

Is it your idea that you live in a cruel and heartless world? Do you have it constructed that Life is against you; that you are simply unappreciated, unrewarded, or even worse, unworthy?

Nothing could be further from the truth. It is, in fact, exactly the opposite. It is *because* you are *deeply* appreciated, *richly* rewarded, and *gloriously* worthy that your life is presenting you with this current Invitation. You have reached Completion before and you have done it again, and now you are being elevated to the next level, as you advance ever onward.

This is The Agenda of the Soul, and this process, Beloved One, is called *evolution*. It is a process of which you are a Living Demonstration.

~

Evolution is not a process that stops. Completion, therefore, does not mean that you have *finished something*.

On The Sacred Journey it is impossible to be "completely Complete" because the instant you reach Completion the Soul conceives of a grander experience yet. This is not, however, a source of frustration. Nor would you ever desire this process to end. The bliss of evolving to higher and higher levels of Divinity is the ultimate attraction. It is the attraction of Life to More Life. It is the attraction of God to God Itself. It is the Impulse of the Divine, in You.

~

The Divine Impulse, your Basic Instinct, is for you to be everything that it is possible for you to be in any given moment. It is the inner feeling that pulls you to the part of You that you are drawn to on every step of the road, every second of your life: the highest truth, the grandest love, the deepest wisdom, the greatest compassion, the largest understanding, the longest patience, the strongest courage—all or any *one* of these aspects of The Divine. And countless other aspects as well, for the Divine is *infinitely* Divine, in an infinite number of ways.

~

You may remember that Chapter 11 was titled "The Most Important Question of Your Life," and it said that this inquiry was: *How does what I am doing right now serve the agenda of my Soul?*

Another version of that same question might be: *How do I choose for Divinity to be expressed through me in the next grandest way in this moment?*

In your answer is found a true act of Creation. In your reply is found a true experience of Free Will. In your response is found God, in the act of being God Itself.

~

God is what you say God is. Love is what you say love is. Truth is what you say truth is. *Nothing has any meaning save the meaning you give it.*

Can you live in such a world, a world without Absolutes? In such a world You are the Determiner. In such a world You are the Decider. In such a world You are the Declarer.

In such a kingdom, you are the Creator.

> *A Soul Knowing:*
> Heaven is not a kingdom where you pay homage to someone else. It is a kingdom where you treat *yourself* as royalty.

This is the Kingdom of Heaven. It is not a kingdom where everything has been decided for you, it is a kingdom where you get to decide about everything. Now that is truly "heaven." It is not a kingdom where you pay homage to someone else. It is a kingdom where you treat *yourself* as royalty.

Can you stand to live in such a kingdom? Can you bear to treat yourself not as The Lowest of the Low, but as The Most High?

Does it sound sacrilegious to even use such a phrase to describe You? Well, here is the Good News: you are *included*, not excluded, from the definition and description of the Most High.

~

In the beginning was the word, and the word was made flesh and dwelt among us. That word has been uttered in hundreds of ways across thousands of moments over a million years and more. Some of those ways: Adonai, Allah, Brahman, Elohim, God, Hari, Jehovah, Krishna, Lord, Rama, Vishnu, Yahweh . . .

. . . and not one of those ways does not include You.

At the beginning of this exploration you were told that you have received a Special Invitation from Life Itself. That Invitation will now be spoken as questions:

Will you allow yourself to re-create yourself anew, in each Golden Moment of Now, in the next grandest version of the greatest vision ever you held about Who You Are?

Will you *consciously* give Divinity the experience of knowing Itself and showing Itself in, as, and through You?

～

"You are goodness and mercy and compassion and understanding. You are peace and joy and light. You are forgiveness and patience, strength and courage, a helper in time of need, a comforter in time of sorrow, a healer in time of injury, a teacher in times of confusion. You are the deepest wisdom and the highest truth; the greatest peace and the grandest love. You *are* these things. And in moments of your life you have known yourself *as* these things. Choose now to know yourself as these things always."

—*Conversations with God, Book 1*

14

The Process, The Path, and The Purpose

THERE IS NO SUGGESTION in all that has been said here, and it should not be implied, that in the process of Divinity Expressing, what one is *doing* is irrelevant or unimportant.

All of Life—including the so-called "spiritual" side of Life—involves "doingness." Everyone is always doing something. It is impossible *not* to be doing something.

Even when you sleep, your Body and Mind are doing something: beating your heart, growing your hair, dreaming your dreams, even sometimes solving your problems.

You are always "up to" something. The question is not, "What are you up to when you are fully conscious and awake?" The question is, "How and Why?"

The answer to that question lies in the perspective you embrace about the reason anything in particular is happening, and the way you're going to play your part in it—even if your part is only that of an observer.

(Actually, there's no such thing as "only" an observer. Quantum physics tells us that "nothing that is observed *is unaffected by the observer.*" This means that even the act of simply observing something in a particular way impacts what is being observed, from near or from afar.)

So whatever you are doing with regard to any situation or during any moment in your life—simply observing or engaging more actively—remember this always: "Doingness" *demonstrates* Who You Are; it does not create it.

In this, most of the human race has it backward.

~

Seeking to experience yourself as Who You Are is The Path of the Soul. Throughout your life you are moving ever and ever closer to Self-Realization. When you demonstrate Who You Are, you achieve Self-Realization and, having reached Completion of the Sacred Journey, your Divine Purpose is fulfilled.

And again, this can occur many times in your life—and does.

You have experienced more than a few moments in which you expressed the qualities of the Divine. Your humility (or your culture) may prohibit you from labeling it as that, or describing it this way, but a rose by any other name is still a rose. You have behaved with utter magnificence on many occasions.

And now, during this unique time in the evolutionary cycle of humanity, and as you move forward with expanded Consciousness in your life, with your sensitivity to *everything* much higher than ever before, it is important to understand that sometimes a demonstration of Divinity may not always look like what you would call the "easiest" path.

As mentioned earlier, some people actually experience more joy, achieve more goals, and work more effectively when facing a major challenge than they do when the going is "easy." In such a case, "easy" may not be "better." It may also not be "faster."

Perhaps Life has already taught you that the shortest route is not necessarily the quickest route.

~

So while The Path of the Soul may not always be the route with the fewest challenges, it will always be the "best" route, given where The Totality of

You is choosing to go, based on where it is right now as a result of all your previous choices and decisions.

The Soul defines "best" as that which is most likely to allow the highest expression of Self that you next choose to experience, based on Life's Divine Purpose.

There is such a purpose, of course. The eternal journey of the Soul, this present Cycle of Life, is not without purpose. There is a *reason* for it occurring.

Life has a reason and a purpose. All people yearn to know what it is. Most have not yet clearly understood.

Your Soul is not on a wild-goose chase. It is not moving through Time and Space forever without a clear objective. Quite to the contrary, the Soul's objective is *very* clear.

Remember that it was said: When *Divine Purpose* has been fulfilled, then your Soul has reached Completion on The Sacred Journey—and this is accomplished in stages.

Let us discuss, then, this thing called Divine Purpose.

~~~

The Divine Purpose is for Life to be used *by* Divinity to *express* Divinity in order *that* Divinity may *experience* Divinity is all of its aspects.

In short, God is using Life in order to experience Itself.

Divinity can be experienced only through the *expression* of it. Divinity can be imagined, it can be thought about, and it can be held in Awareness by the Soul, but until it is *expressed*, it is merely a concept; unless it is *expressed*, it cannot be experienced.

> A Soul Knowing:
> Until you *express*
> Divinity you cannot
> experience Divinity.

You can talk about Love, you can imagine Love, you can think about Love, you can hold Love as an idea conceptually, but until you *express* it, you cannot experience it.

You can talk about Compassion, you can imagine Compassion, you can think about Compassion, you can hold Compassion as an idea conceptually, but until you *express* it, you cannot experience it.

You can talk about Understanding, you can imagine Understanding, you can think about Understanding, you can hold Understanding as an idea conceptually, but until you *express* it, you cannot experience it.

You can talk about Forgiveness, you can imagine Forgiveness, you can think about Forgiveness, you can hold Forgiveness as an idea conceptually, but until you *express* it, you cannot experience it.

～

To help the Mind better grasp this, let's use that aspect of human life called Sexuality. You can talk about Sexuality, you can imagine Sexuality, you can think about Sexuality, you can hold Sexuality as an idea conceptually, but until you *express* it, you cannot experience it.

Divinity is all of these things, and much more. It is Patience and Kindness, Goodness and Mercy, Acceptance and Forbearance, Wisdom and Clarity, Gentleness and Beauty, Selflessness and Nobility, Benevolence and Generosity. And yes, much, much more.

You can imagine all of these things, you can think about all of these things, you can hold all of these things as ideas conceptually, but until you *express* all of these things *in* you, *through* you, *as* you, you have not experienced Divinity.

And you will never have an opportunity to experience these things unless Life *provides* you with such an opportunity. This is what Life is doing every day. Indeed, this is the purpose of Life Itself.

Therefore, when Life brings you challenges, difficulties, and unique conditions, situations, and circumstances that are ideally suited to bring out the best in you, "judge not, and neither condemn," but be a Light unto the darkness, that you might know Who You Really Are—and that all those whose lives you touch might know who they are as well, by the light of your example.

⌒

While the idea that "God uses Life to know Godself" is surely not new to you, *why* God works this way may very well be something you'd like to know more about.

So here is the explanation.

God cannot experience all that God is within the Spiritual Realm alone, because in that realm there is nothing that God is not.

The Realm of the Spiritual is the place where God is all there *is*, where Love is all there *is*, where Perfection is all there *is*. It's a wonderful place, because there is nothing but Divinity. It is, in short, what you would call heaven.

There is, however, this particular reality: There is nothing that God is not. And in the absence of what God is *not*, what God is . . . is not *experienceable*.

⌒

The same is true about you. You cannot experience what *you* are except in the presence of What You Are Not. Nor is *anything* able to be experienced unless it is in a Contextual Field that includes its opposite.

The light cannot be experienced without the darkness. "Up" has no meaning in experience without "down." "Fast" is simply a term, a word having no meaning whatsoever without "slow."

Only in the presence of the thing called "small" can the thing called "big" be experienced. We can *say* that something is "big," we can *imagine* that something is "big," we can *conceptualize* something as being "big," but in the absence of something that is "small," "big" cannot be experienced.

Likewise, in the absence of something "finite," "infinity" cannot be experienced. Put into theological terms, we can know "Divinity" *conceptually*, but we cannot know it *experientially*.

Therefore, all the people and events of your life—now or in the past—which seem to be "at odds" with who you are and what you choose to experience, are simply gifts from the highest source, created for you and brought to you through the collaborative process of co-creating souls, allowing you to find yourself in a Contextual Field within which the fullest experience of Who You Really Are becomes possible.

Or, as it was so wonderfully stated by The Divine in *Conversations with God:*

I have sent you nothing but angels.

Now there's a statement to remember.

It was said here that your eternal Sacred Journey has a purpose, and it does indeed. It is a purpose established by Divinity Itself.

The Divine Purpose is to expand the Reality of God.

In simple terms (and these *are* simple terms), God is growing—becoming more of Itself—through the process called Life. God IS this process.

God is both the Process of Life Itself . . . and the result of it.

Thus, God is The Creator and The Created. The Alpha and the Omega. The Beginning and The End. The Unmoved Mover. The Unwatched Watcher.

In not so simple terms, God cannot "grow" because everything that God ever was, is now, or ever will be, Is Now.

There is no Time and there is no Space. Therefore, there is no time in which to grow, and no space *into* which to grow.

The Cycle of Life is occurring simultaneously everywhere. What the human Mind wants to call God's "growth" is merely God experiencing more and more of Itself as the Individuations of God experience more and more of *them*selves. This is called Evolution.

This was accomplished by The Whole dividing Itself (not to be confused with *separating* Itself) *from* Itself, re-creating Itself in smaller and finite form.

No finite form, by the very reason of its being finite, could hold the infinite consciousness, awareness, and experience of The Whole, yet each individuated form was designed uniquely to reflect a particular *aspect* of Divinity Itself. Putting all these aspects together again, as one puts the pieces of a puzzle together, produces a picture of what *all the pieces create.*

Namely: God.

All the pieces are part of the picture, and no piece is less a part of the picture than any other.

Get the picture?

~

Now some forms of Life have been endowed with a level of Essential Essence (the raw energy from which everything springs) sufficient to produce the possibility of that Essence *knowing Itself.*

This is the quality in certain living things that is called Self-Consciousness.

Human Life (and, we suspect with good reason, Life elsewhere in the Universe) was designed in such a way that what we call "expansion" of Consciousness and Experience is possible. In fact, human Consciousness can expand even to a point where it once again knows itself as part of The Whole.

Jesus, for instance, said: *I and the Father are one.* He understood his relationship to God perfectly. He understood that the picture which the puzzle created was not Complete without him. He *was* The Completion.

As are we all.

> *A Soul Knowing:*
> God is both the
> Process of Life Itself
> and the result of it.

Take one piece of the puzzle away and the picture is not Complete.

The experience of becoming fully Self Consciousness occurs through a process by which the Individuated Aspect does not *grow,* actually, but simply becomes more and more *aware* that it does not *have* to grow, but truly is, in its individuated form, Divinity Itself.

The individual piece recognizes itself as The Puzzle Itself, simply divided.

The spectacular physiological, psychological, and theological transition into that higher level of Self-Awareness occurs *only once* in the epochal history of every sentient species in the cosmos—and this is precisely what is happening within the human race right now.

In the very first chapter of this book we said: "Something very unusual is occurring on this planet right now." We weren't kidding.

15

How It All Works

THE STORY OF HUMANITY'S birthing into the cosmic community of Highly Evolved Beings is already complete, etched into EverMoment.

All has already occurred in that place of Time/No time. It is only the re-witnessing of The Story, with the eyes of our own Consciousness gazing upon it, that is awaited. It is us, bearing witness, that makes the story's unfoldment real to us.

~

To fully understand the above, hold a DVD of your favorite movie in your hand. Notice that *the entire movie already exists* on the disc.

When you put the DVD into a player and watch the story unfold, even you know that everything has already happened. The disc player isn't creating the story as it goes along, it is simply accessing the story that has already been created. It is projecting a miniscule portion of *what is all there in whole and complete form* onto your viewing screen frame by frame. This makes it *appear* as if it's actually *happening* frame by frame, even though you know in truth that it's all already on the disc, right to the story's very end.

You can hit Fast Forward and actually watch the story unfold rapidly, no longer in real time (as you understand "real time"). In real life, we all know how "time flies" when you're having fun.

Conversely, you can observe the story on the disc in slow motion—and many are those who will swear to you that they have watched a critical Moment in their own lives happening *as if everything had slowed down.*

That's as close as this narrative can come to explaining, using a simple illustration that the Mind easily embraces, exactly what is going on in Life.

So know this: Everything that ever was, is now, and ever will be . . . *is now.* The Universe is full of stories, everything already having played out, all simply waiting for our witnessing of it.

Do you wish to know this in real terms? Look up at the night sky. You are looking at what has already happened. The twinkling stars did their twinkling years ago—*light*-years ago. *Do you think this is happening Right Now?* You are looking at *what has already occurred.*

Millennia ago.

This is how you know, by the way, that nothing bad is going to happen on planet Earth. By that is meant nothing completely, totally, and utterly disastrous, at the level of planetary calamity. We're not going to be blasted out of the sky by a meteor, nor will our species be rendered extinct by some other galactic cataclysm. If this were to happen, *it would have already happened,* and *we wouldn't be here to watch it in human form.*

The fact that we are here to watch Life is our evidence that Life goes on. The only reason this may not be obvious to you is if you think there is a "future." Yet the "future" is Now. There is only This Moment. So if our "future" held our demise, This Moment would not exist!

~

Wouldn't it be ironic if a microscopic view of a DVD from its curved edge revealed a conglomeration of submolecular particles on a disc that looked exactly like a swirling galaxy?

Is it so wild to imagine that the Milky Way is but one of a million DVDs (Divine Visions Demonstrated) in God's "home movie collection"?

Have a hard time going there? Fair enough. That may be a bit fanciful. At least the wording of it, if not the physics. Yet you might be intrigued by this: physicists declare that the entire universe can be explained by mathematical formulas. And you already know now that all that is on a video disc is *digital data*. That is, *mathematics*. Not pictures, but digits that, by their sequencing and formula, *produce* pictures.

And if that doesn't intrigue you, try this from William Shakespeare:

> *There are more things in heaven and earth, Horatio,*
> *than are dreamt of in your philosophy.*
>
> "Hamlet"
> Act I, Scene V

~

(Publisher's Note: Portions of the DVD analogy first appeared in print in *The Storm Before the Calm,* Hay House 2011, the initial entry in the Conversations of Humanity Series, of which this is the second. Taken together, the two books offer a here-and-now invitation to create a brand new human story, with many ideas on how every single person can alter the creation of individual and collective experience.)

~

Now, what good does it do for you to know that everything that ever was, is now, and ever will happen is now? Other than as esoteric knowledge, does that information have any value?

Yes. It allows us to know that everything will turn out alright *no matter how it turns out*. The proof of that is that you are *still here*, witnessing your present "playing out" of this "drama."

Let's use your imagination once more. Imagine you are in a movie studio's vaulted library, looking at old movies that were still made on celluloid. And suppose (and, by the way, this is not at all outside the realm of things possible) that you had a chance to view reels of different "takes" of classic scenes—takes not included in the film you first saw—including reels of entirely different *alternate endings.*

Or imagine that you're sitting in the back row of a darkened theater on Broadway. It is two weeks after the opening of a major play, and both the playwright and the director are experimenting with different ways of playing a scene that has not been working as they would like it.

Now imagine that your own life is exactly like that. Imagine that a scene has not been working as you would like it. Wouldn't it be wonderful to have a chance to play the scene again, a different way?

Well, the fact that is revealed in the "esoteric knowledge" previously derived from the previous DVD illustration is that you *do* have the chance to play the scene again. Every scene. Or any particular scene, or *kind of scene,* that you wish.

You want to redo a scene of betrayal? A scene of anger? A scene of self-discovery? A scene of failure? A scene of great joy, not fully realized?

You may play any scene or type of scene over and over again, as often as you wish. *That* is the purpose of knowing about the fact that everything that ever was, is now, and ever will be *is now.* All the possibilities in the Universe exist simultaneously, and you get to decide which ones you wish to experience *this time through the scene.*

Have you not ever had the experience of being overcome with a feeling that, "Oh, my God, I've *been here before*"?

Déjà vu, from the French, literally "already seen," is the phenomenon of believing an event or experience has occurred in the past. It has.

Thinking of your life as a play, with you as the lead character, may be new to you, but it was not new to Mr. Shakespeare, the master playwright we quoted earlier. Said he . . .

All the world's a stage,
And all the men and women merely players:
They have their exits and their entrances;
And one man in his time plays many parts.

"As You Like It"
Act II Scene VII

Now let's look at how one scene from life might play itself out in your own day-to-day experience.

Here is an example . . .

Let's say that Divine Purpose at a particular moment is to experience, through you, that aspect of Divinity which you call "patience."

> *A Soul Knowing:*
> Everything that ever was, is now, and ever will be, *is now.*

In such an instance would it be more *purposeful* for your Soul, as the agent of the Divine, to create a moment or an hour or a day in which everything was going perfectly and not a stitch of patience was required? Or, in the alternative, would it be more purposeful to collaborate with other souls in the co-creation of a situation, condition, event, or circumstance in which you had an opportunity to *demonstrate patience*—and thus, *experience* it and *become* it?

Ah! says the Mind, *I see.*

And so we observe that Divine Purpose may not always involve the Soul taking what you would call the easiest path. Still, the Path of the Soul will always be the *simplest* path, and the *fastest* path, to experience Completion of the Sacred Journey. You can choose to play the scenes in your life any way that you wish. You can choose the "easiest" path (in the case above, no scenes that require "patience"), or you can choose the "fastest" path. With regard to how you play all the scenes in your life, you may have it as you like it.

In the end you will find that the fastest path will also be the most joyous path—precisely because answering the biggest challenge produces the biggest reward. And it is a function of life to place a challenge before you. Not difficulty, mind you. Simply challenge. The word "challenge" is not synonymous with the word "struggle." The first need not produce the second.

Indeed, here is a dictionary definition that you might find interesting: *Challenge:* "A query as to the truth of something, often with an implicit invitation for proof."

So the challenges in your life are not meant to be struggles, they are meant to be *questions.* And the highest challenge asks the biggest question: What is the truth of who you are? What is the proof?

Every thought you embrace, every word you speak, every action you take is your answer. It is your Truth About Yourself, *and your proof of it.*

16

Eliminating Life's Complexity

Now there is something very important you must know and understand, or this part of your exploration could become very discouraging.

An old human view and a traditional religious view (explored in the book *What God Wants*) is that God's desire is for suffering to be used by human beings to better themselves and to purify their soul. Suffering is good. It earns credits, or points, in God's mind, especially if it's endured silently, and maybe even "offered up" to God.

Suffering is a necessary part of human growth and learning and is, more importantly, a means by which people may be redeemed in the eyes of God.

Indeed, one whole religion is built on this belief, asserting that all beings have been saved by the suffering of one being, who died for the sins of the rest. This one being paid the "debt" said to be owed to God for humanity's weakness and wickedness.

According to this doctrine, God has been hurt by the weakness and wickedness of humanity and, in order to set things straight, *someone has to suffer.* Otherwise, God and humanity could not be reconciled. Thus, suffering was established as a redemptive experience.

With regard to the suffering of human beings due to "natural" causes, it's not to be shortened by death under any circumstances that are not also "natural." The suffering of animals may be mercifully ended before "natural" death, but not the suffering of people. It's God and God alone who determines when human suffering shall end.

One result of this teaching: Human beings have endured unimaginable suffering over extended periods in order to do God's will and not incur God's wrath in the afterlife. Millions of people feel that even if a person is very, very old and is suffering very, very much—lingering on the verge of death but not dying, experiencing interminable pain instead—that person must endure whatever life is bringing them.

Humanity has actually created civil law declaring that people have no right to end their own suffering, nor may they assist others in ending theirs. However anguishing it may be, however otherwise hopeless a life may have become, the suffering must go on.

This is, the orthodox view tells us, *what God wants.*

Now, in what some like to think of as an enlightened age, many people (but by no means all) have rejected these notions. However, a large number have replaced them with *new* thoughts that are not much better, suggesting that humanity's innate desire to experience Divinity can only be satisfied by *suffering through* what humanity experiences to be the opposite of Divinity.

In fact, after reading the item near the closing of the previous chapter *right here,* one could imagine a person becoming quite angry, saying: "Are you telling me that if God wants to experience the Divine Quality called 'patience,' I have to suffer through everything that creates that opportunity? Are you saying that I have to keep suffering *all* the difficult and trying conditions in my life simply so that God can *know Itself?* Excuse me, but *no thanks!*"

So before you go too far down that road, this Official Notice please; this note from the Front Office:

GOD IS NOT ASKING YOU TO BE A SURROGATE SUFFERER.

That is very important to hold in Consciousness, lest you find yourself embracing the notion that you are experiencing struggling and suffering *as a response to God's desire* to experience Divinity.

If you experience struggle and suffering it is not because you have responded to God's desire, but because you have forgotten it.

~

God's Greatest Desire is to experience Divinity in its Fullest Form. That Fullest Form does not include struggle and suffering. You are not required to experience negativity in any form in order for God to experience Divinity in every form.

The emotions that produce struggle and suffering are products of the human Mind. God does not label any condition "bad," or become "aggravated" or "offended" or "frustrated" because a particular circumstance has arisen.

God understands that everything arising is an invitation for Divinity to express itself at its next highest level.

You may understand this, too, at a theoretical level, yet even though you are a Divine being, you are not all that God is, and so of course it is understandable that while God does not experience suffering, you may.

A drop of the ocean is water, for sure, but it is not The Ocean. Yet compared to a submolecular particle, a drop of water might as well *be* The Ocean—such is its relative size and power as it rolls through a submolecular particle field. And as the drop of water is to the ocean, so are you to God. This means that you have Divine Power proportionate to your size. And *that* means that you possess Divine Power *proportionate to your problems.*

This may be the most important information you will ever receive.

The problems that each of us face every day, considered within the entire Contextual Field in which God exists, are surely minuscule. Indeed, within that context they are not "problems" at all, but merely "conditions." Yet for every one of us our biggest problems feel, understandably (and appropriately), very large. They are, after all, being encountered by *us;* they are not being encountered by God.

Or are they . . . ?

What if it were God who *was* encountering these conditions, *through* us?

If God lives in us, that would be true. And God *does* live within us, so it *is* true.

The message here is that we are larger than we think—and our problems are smaller in relationship to us than we imagine. Mystics and sages have said for ages that life never sends us a problem too large for us to handle. They are right. And *groups* of us, working together, have enough power to overcome every problem that groups of us have created. All we have to do is *decide to.*

And so in our own personal space, and in the environment collectively created by the lot of us, we are, in a sense, Deities, even as a drop of water is an "ocean" in the space of a submolecular particle.

—

The immense power that is yours has to do with the tools you have been given with which to create the experiences of your life. With these tools, you can end suffering in your personal life forever and eliminate struggle from your encounters.

These tools are shared in Part Three of this book, where we look at how The Only Thing That Matters may be applied in a practical way every day.

> *A Soul Knowing:*
> You possess Divine Power proportionate to your problems.

For now, allow yourself to know that your Soul experiences all of Life's Moments entirely different from the way your Mind experiences them. So you will not find these powerful tools in your Mind's array of resources.

At least, not at first. Not until you have trained your Mind to include your Soul in your consideration of everything that is happening around you. Then your Mind can utilize these tools in the face of any exterior circumstance, past or present, that invites your next demonstration of Divinity.

Now once again let it be said that moving into such a demonstration is not required. You do not have to do this. It is not demanded of you.

You can choose for the expression and the experiencing of Divinity to be the purpose of any given Moment in your life, or not, as you wish. Nothing "bad" will happen to you at the end of your present life on Earth if you do not. The choice is entirely yours. Many of the planet's theologies describe this choice as Free Will.

~~~

There is a reason that nothing bad will happen to you if you do not choose to express Divinity in your life—a reason that most of Earth's theologies reject. The reason is that you cannot *fail* to express Divinity, no matter *what* you do.

Now remember when you were invited here to have patience? Please exercise patience once again. We are venturing further into this spiritual complexity now because understanding this can help you eliminate much of the complexity of human life.

Having said that, be advised that what you are about to read *may be the single most difficult concept about Life and God that humanity has ever been invited to embrace.*

~~~

The only way that a human being could fail to express Divinity would be for a human thought, word, or action to be other than Divine, and *such a thing is impossible.* It is life's Great Impossibility.

In physical life there are *forms* of Divinity—some complete, some incomplete; some pure, some distorted—but there is no such thing as an *absence* of Divinity.

For there to be an absolute absence of Divinity, life on Earth would have to be separate from, or "other than," That Which Is Divine. Yet physical life is *not* separate from The Divine, nor can it be, since it is, in its entirety, an expression *of* The Divine.

God therefore sees nothing that is not Divine—even if it appears in distorted form. In physical life, which is experienced in relative terms, there is no such thing as an absence of Divinity—but there are degrees of It.

It might help you to think of this as degrees of purity. Imagine placing food coloring, one drop at a time, into a large pitcher of the purest water from the clearest mountain stream. Because a drop of food coloring has been placed into the water does not mean that the pitcher does not contain mountain water; it means that the mountain water is now not quite pure. The more drops of coloring you place in the water, the less pure the water that fills the pitcher will be—but it will still and always be mountain water.

The more Thoughts you hold that are limited to the Mind's Experience rather than including the Soul's Awareness, the less pure will be the energy that fills your being. Yet that energy will still and always be the Essence of the Divine.

Or think of a mirror in a frame that has been slightly twisted to produce a distorted reflection, as in a carnival fun house. The image is distorted to the degree that the reflecting surface has been warped, but the being in the mirror is still, and will always be, *you.* Your image can be distorted, but it cannot be anything *but* your image, *distorted.*

~

Now let's see if we can come up with an example that places this concept "on the ground" in everyday life. Once again, let's use a common experience.

Fear.

All fear (and that which derives from it, such as anger, hatred, and violence) is a distorted form of love.

That's an important statement, and you should read it again.

If you think about it, you will realize that if a person loved nothing, that person would be totally free of fear, anger, hatred, or violence, because there would be no *need* for such emotions to arise—nor the actions that proceed from them.

Exploring this further, we see that fear, anger, hatred, and violence are expressions of the *loss,* or the *anticipated* loss, of something which is loved. Or, of *never having to begin with* something which is loved.

If there is no love of anything, there is no sense of loss or deprivation, and therefore no negative emotion of any kind attached to the absence of anything. Do you see this?

Because humans, in their limited perspective, misunderstand how to express their love, they behave in ways that appear to be the opposite of love—but which are, in fact, distorted *wailings* of love.

All expressions of anger and fear, hatred and violence are distorted wailings of Love. Remember that. For the rest of your life, remember that.

The person who grasps this, grasps at the edges of Divinity.

~

Where Divinity expresses, forgiveness is never necessary, for it is rendered pointless in the presence of absolute understanding—which is, of course, what Divinity *is.*

This was the whole point of the biblical story of Jesus forgiving the thief on the cross next to him.

Jesus, in his absolute understanding, recognized that the thief acted out of his love for something when he stole and simply expressed that love in a distorted form.

And, of course, there was no place other than heaven for the thief to go to in any case. Precisely because God perfectly understands everyone and everything, God has no need to create a place of eternal damnation, indescribable suffering, unspeakable torment, and unending torture. *Heaven is all there is,* and that paradise includes life on Earth.

~

If we do not experience life on Earth as a paradise, it is because we have not yet understood the true purpose of Life Itself, or how to manifest it in and through our daily lives. Yet evolution is the process by which all sentient beings come to that understanding, and evolution will not be denied.

Evolution's extraordinary insight is that the worst crimes and behaviors of humans will never be forgiven by God.

Never.

Not because God refuses to forgive, but because *absolution is not necessary,* since all human action is based, at its root, in love, however confused, mistaken, or distorted its expression.

As *Conversations with God* puts it: No one does anything inappropriate, given their model of the world.

> *A Soul Knowing:*
> All fear is but a distorted form of Love.

The healing message of that dialogue is simple: Evolution is not a sin, and God does not punish confusion.

17

Putting It All Together

"God may not punish confusion, but God does punish disobedience. It is one thing to say you just didn't know, but it is another thing to be told, outright, what is so and then completely ignore it."

You may have heard those words before. They spell out the fundamental principle, the foundational basis, of most of the world's major religions. If you've read this far in this book and embraced its ideas, you are in deep trouble, these belief systems tell you. They tell you that God and Life are not One, but that God *created* Life, and Man as a part of Life in God's Image and Likeness, but that—image and likeness or not—Man cannot become God, and must not attempt to *be* God, lest Man commit the greatest sin, for which condemnation to eternal damnation *is,* absolutely and without a doubt, the punishment.

This, these belief systems teach us, was the great sin of Satan—and it is the sin that Satan is trying to get *us* to commit, so that we will join him in perdition. Satan is doing this, apparently, to get *back* at God for sending *him* to that awful place. Satan wants to "rob" God of His Souls by claiming them as Satan's own, so that he can punish God for himself having been punished.

You may have heard commentaries such as this regarding the doctrines of some organized religions before, but it may be useful now to look beneath the dogma to what generated the idea of Right and Wrong/Good and Evil in those doctrines in the first place.

The dogma surrounding "sin" is based on the theological doctrine of Separation. That doctrine *must be held firmly in place* or the construct of "sin" dissolves.

Religions understand this. That is why many religions teach that God is "over there" and Man is "over here," and never the two shall meet, except on Judgment Day, when—even though you are not supposed to try to be God—you will, in fact, be judged on how much *like* God you have behaved.

Humans are told to be *like* God, but that they have to do so without *being* God. They are told that they are made in the image and likeness of God, but they do not have the abilities of God. So they are consigned to failure before they begin in this business of being as much like God as they can be.

> *A Soul Knowing:*
> Life invites you
> always to live the
> life that you were
> designed to live.

Still, God will forgive them for their failures if they will try. But if they do *not* try, or if they try but fail miserably and in the worst possible way, God will judge them, condemn them, and punish them to everlasting torture and pain.

This is human theology—most of it—in a nutshell. There are variations on the theme, but that is the gist of it.

⌇

There's no point in going any further with this. Hundreds of other books have been written on the subject. But now, consider this: If separation from God is *not* the Ultimate Reality, if God's revealed *identity* as That-Which-Created-Life, But-Which-Is-'Other-Than'-Life is *not the true state of things,* then the basis of most human theologies is faulty; their doctrines crumble.

Should humanity choose to lay aside the Doctrine of Separation, life on Earth could be lived according to a New Theology, in a new way: not as an attempt to *get back to God in heaven,* but to *get back to creating heaven on Earth;* not as an effort to make sure we are not excluded from God's Kingdom, but as an effort to make sure that God's Kingdom is not excluded from *us*—and to make sure that this whole *place* (called Earth) is treated as *part* of that Kingdom.

Ironically, this would be achieved by us being as much like God as we can be. So, here is the Supreme Irony: First we are told that Satan was punished for thinking that he was Divine, then we are told that we were made "in the image and likeness of God" and that *we* will be punished if we do *not* behave in Godly fashion.

The theology of our ancestors has us coming and going, and the human species is now facing a future-creating choice: Old Theology or New Theology; Yesterday's God or Tomorrow's God.

The second choice offers Life's most tantalizing enticement ever: to live the life you were *designed* to live, to experience your Self in your truest form, to express the Essence of Who You Really Are in the next grandest way.

This is not something that is outside the capability of humans. "Regular people" just like you have done this. Remember, what is being talked about here is expressing Divinity in the next grandest way, and that is an ongoing, expanding process.

The good news is that even expressing a tiny *portion* of Divinity can change one's life so dramatically that struggle and suffering, anxiety and worry, fear and anger, grief and misery can be removed from one's daily encounters forever.

～

Completion of the *entire* process of Divine Experience Through Expression in the Realm of the Physical is impossible due to the limitation of physicality itself—a point made in Chapter 14 discussing the finite nature of our lives. Yet in the Totality of the three-part Kingdom of God (the Realm of *Physicality* plus the Realm of the *Spirituality* plus the Realm of *Pure Being*) the Totality of Divinity *can* be known, expressed, and experienced by the Totality of You.

This impossibility of Completion of The Sacred Journey *in its entirety* during one physical lifetime is what standard theology has correctly understood, but incorrectly taught. It has attempted in good faith to teach it, but it has done so in an inaccurate and damaging way. It has done so by sharing as dogma a doctrine of Separation from God, rather than by sharing as a celebration the truth of the Magnificence of God.

It is because we are all united with a Divinity so utterly *magnificent* and *limitless* that we need more than one lifetime to experience it! It is *not* because all things physical are separate from God, but exactly the opposite.

As we've already explained, using our stage-play illustration, it may take many passes through a single lifetime (sometimes producing, as we discussed a bit ago, the experience of *déjà vu*), and passages through hundreds of separate lifetimes (does *reincarnation* sound familiar?) for a Soul to be "completely" Complete! All of which brings us back down to you, the individual expression of the Divine that is undertaking this self-exploration by reading this book right now. What does any of this have to do with helping you to focus, on this day of your life, on The Only Thing That Matters?

> *A Soul Knowing:*
> It is because we are all united with a Divinity so utterly *magnificent* and *limitless* that we need more than one lifetime to experience it!

Well, we have made the point from the outset that it's important to understand how something *works* before you can understand why it is *not* working. The narrative here has been leading you, step-by-step, through the blueprint of Life, reminding your Mind of what your Soul knows about how things were designed to work. In summary then, here is that data, condensed.

～

The Grand Design is this: God created physicality as the means by which to express Its Totality in relative terms, so that It might experience Divinity in all of Its aspects.

The Blueprint of Physical Human Life is this: You are a three-part being, made up of Body, Mind, and Soul. There is no separation within this triad, which has here been called "The Totality of You." The Totality of You is, in fact, an individuation of Divinity Itself. Even as Divinity is a Triune (BEING, KNOWING, EXPERIENCING), so, too, are you (SOUL, MIND, BODY). You *are,* just as it has been said in many theological circles, made in the image and likeness of God.

The Agenda of the Soul is this: To express and experience every aspect of its True Identity as an Individuation of Divinity by reaching Completion of The Sacred Journey in moment-to-moment expressions of Life; to collaboratively create, with other souls, the right and perfect conditions, situations, and circumstances within which it becomes possible to experience this.

The Sacred Journey is this: an ongoing, eternal expression by the Soul of the Essential or Primal Energy called Life, in specific and particular forms, fulfilling The Divine Purpose by means of physicalizations, which are referred to in human terms as "lifetimes."

The Divine Purpose is this: Continual Completion. That is, the complete experience of Divinity in any and every one of its aspects through ongoing physical expressions reflecting the Nature of the Divine insofar as any physical manifestation is capable of doing so at any particular evolutionary stage.

～

When a flower blooms, Divine Purpose (the expression and experience of any aspect of Divinity) has been fulfilled—and The Sacred Journey of the life form called "flower" has reached Completion at that stage. It does not reach what would be called "total" Completion, because the life form called "flower" does not and cannot ever "die" or "go away." Its energy simply changes form, moving to the next stage in its expression and manifestation.

When a tree grows to its highest point, ultimately falling of its own weight, Divine Purpose (the expression and experience of any aspect of Divinity) has been fulfilled—and The Sacred Journey of the life form called "tree" has reached Completion at that stage. It does not reach what would be called "total" Completion, because the life form called "tree" does not and cannot ever "die" or "go away." Its energy simply changes form, moving to the next stage in its expression and manifestation.

When a human being expresses fully, Divine Purpose (the expression and experience of any aspect of Divinity) has been fulfilled—and The Sacred Journey of the life form called "human" has reached Completion at that stage. It does not reach what would be called "total" Completion, because the life form called "human" does not and cannot ever "die" or "go away." When a particular life span is over, a human being does exactly the same thing that other Life Forms do: Its energy changes form, moving to the next stage in its expression and manifestation.

Unlike flowers or trees or other less developed biological Life Forms, the Life Expression called human beings is capable of expressing and experiencing wisdom—specifically, the Wisdom of the Soul—through which, when added to the Experience held in the Mind, a state of "partial Completion" may be reached many, many times, during many moments, across one physical life span.

To finish the moment, to find
the journey's end in every step of the road,
to live the greatest number of good hours,
is wisdom.

—Ralph Waldo Emerson

Humans have reached a level of Awareness that may be the highest of any Life Form on the Earth. (We imagine ourselves to be more advanced than dolphins or whales and most other Life Forms—but this is by no means certain.)

As explained early in this exploration, your Life Form is now reaching a new level of Consciousness as a result of the Mind now paying much more attention to the Awareness of the Soul—even as a primitive human at some point became aware that the reflection seen in the water was the Self.

Through the process in which you have engaged right here on these pages, you have seen your own reflection and recognized it as your Self.

To use the Life Path Metaphor one last time: It is when your Mind and your Body deviate from The Path of the Soul that the Mind forgets. And the Body and the Mind are not *required* to follow the Path of the Soul, as has been explained, and so can be lured by other attractions. Yet, now expanding on the metaphor, there is a safety device built into this process—a device that guarantees that you will eventually make it safely to the top of the mountain. Like all good mountain climbers, the three parts of The Totality of You are tethered. (Some spiritual teachers call this connection a "silver cord.")

The connecting cord is very long, so the Mind and the Body can stray far, far from the Soul before the line becomes taut. (It could be said that God has given you "plenty of rope.") But at some point, the line becomes stretched and tight. It is then that you begin to feel that You are being pulled in three different directions.

Everyone has experienced this feeling. You may be feeling this way right now. If you are, it is because you have left The Path of the Soul. But don't worry. You're on your way back to the path. And this time, you'll have a map showing you how to *stay on the path*.

Because this time you are going to know about The Only Thing That Matters.

18

The Map

AND SO WE COME TO THE BOTTOM LINE. Having looked at Life and its Divine Purpose, having described in metaphor The Sacred Journey, having explained in detail The Agenda of the Soul, and having defined the very nature of The Totality of You, we arrive at the question with which our exploration began: What *is* The Only Thing That Matters?

The answer will form the foundation of every day, every hour, every minute of your life. This answer will impact everything you think and say and do. This answer will affect the quality of your life from morning til night.

This answer will determine how successful you are—and what you define as "success." This answer will determine how healthy you are—and what you define as "health." This answer will determine how loved and loving you are—and what you define as "love."

This answer will literally create your relationships—both your intimate, romantic relationships and your relationships with family, friends, and everybody in your exterior world. This answer will produce what you do to make a living and what you do to make a life. This answer will affect how you spend time with those you care for, and what you do when you are alone.

This answer will affect *everything,* your entire life, from this moment until the moment you die. It will even affect *how* you die.

The Only Thing That Matters is so important that everything else pales by comparison to it, shrinks to irrelevance in the face of it, and is probably only in place to *begin* with because of it.

Your entire past is a reflection of The Only Thing That Matters, and your entire future will be created by it.

So here it is. In this life on Earth, this is The Only Thing That Matters:

What One Desires

∼

Now that may not be at all what you expected. Yet one's commitment to always and evermore seek to announce and declare, to know and express, to experience and fulfill only What One Desires lies at the core of your ability to serve The Agenda of the Soul, to reach Completion on The Sacred Journey, and to achieve The Divine Purpose.

Your decision to do this is the most powerful decision you will ever make. And what renders it more critical than it might at first appear is the fact that it is not a decision you make once and then live with. It is a decision that you make every second of every minute of every hour of every day. Indeed, you have been making this decision since you were old enough to think about it.

But you have probably been thinking about it in the wrong way.

And that is what Part Three of this book is all about.

It is about What One Desires—and what that really means.

∼

Get ready.

It is not what you think.

Part Three

A description of what it looks like
to walk the Path of the Soul,
and an offering of extraordinary tools for
focusing the entirety of your life on
The Only Thing That Matters.

19

Should One Really Spend a Lifetime Catering Only to One's Desire?

DEAR FRIEND . . . If you jumped ahead to Part Three, you will need to at least go back a few page turns and read the last chapter. If you came to this place in the text by way of reading all of Part Two, you know now that The Only Thing That Matters is What One Desires.

Yet could this possibly be true? Is it really our conclusion, after this long and deep exploration into the most important thing in Life, that the most important thing in Life is *one's own desires*?

Yes, it could be true and it is true. Furthermore, most people already know this. The problem is not that people don't know that The Only Thing That Matters is What One Desires, but that they have been *thinking about it in the wrong way.*

Most people think that focusing on What One Desires means focusing on themselves. It means just the opposite. Yet how could any of us know this when everything in our culture, in our upbringing, and in our social interactions has led us right straight to massive misunderstanding?

Even those who have rejected modern society's orthodoxy of Bigger/ Better/More, stepped aside from its indoctrinations, and eschewed its traditions and conventions by turning to "alternative" lifestyles and beliefs have heard from the mouths of their new teachers, ministers, and healers *the exact same message:* You can have anything you desire by using The Power Within You!

It's true! Have you seen the movie? There was a movie made about this very subject not long ago. It was all about how we can use a fundamental law of the Universe, the creative energy that it calls the Law of Attraction, to magnetize and attract to ourselves anything that our hearts desire—and about how this power has largely been keep a secret from us for thousands of years by those few who knew about it.

> *A Soul Knowing:*
> The Only Thing
> That Matters is
> What One Desires.

At last, the film proclaims, this formula has been revealed, and now *everyone* can have What One Desires!

And what is it that was depicted as What One Desires?

The film shows a man walking to his driveway and finding the car he has always dreamt of owning; a woman blinking in delighted surprise as a bejeweled necklace appears like magic on her bodice; even a small boy ecstatic at his discovery of a shiny new bicycle outside the front door, waiting just for him.

Not a word about how—if we truly *have* all this power—we could produce world peace. Or end global hunger. Or heal planetary suffering.

Not a word.

And it's not the filmmaker's fault. They were merely reflecting the priorities of humanity's culture. These have even become the priorities of our so-called "New Age."

This is the culture into which most of us have been thrust, and in which most of us continue to be submerged. Small wonder we are confused about The Only Thing That Matters.

~

Now comes a book by that very title, offering to help end our confusion—yet attempting to do so by telling us, *one more time,* what everyone else has been telling us all along . . . !

The Only Thing That Matters is What One Desires.

But wait. Hold it. There's more. There's more to be said here about What One Desires.

At higher levels of Consciousness those three words take on a much deeper meaning. When you are fully awake, you find that "What One Desires" refers not to your personal desires, but to the desires of The One.

Then, at even higher levels of Consciousness, you find that *the two are One and The Same.* Your personal desires and the desires of The One are *identical.*

"The One"?

Yes, *The One.*

~

All things are One Thing. There is only One Thing, and all things are part of the One Thing There Is.

This One Thing has been called by many names. It has been called Life. It has been called The Essential Essence. It has been called The Energy. It has been called Allah, Brahma, Divinity, Elohim, God, Jehovah, and a host of other names as well. It does not matter what name you use. It is the only thing there is, and you are part of it.

Because you are an integral part of it, it is only natural that what you want at the heart of your being is what it wants at the core of its existence.

For the purposes of the discussion here we've been referring to The One Thing There Is with the word "Divinity," and occasionally with the word "God."

~

Divinity has only one desire, and that is to experience Itself fully through the complete Knowing and Expression of Itself.

Life is Its achievement of exactly that. No particular *part* of Life, but *all of Life put together.* It is the *sum and the substance* of Life aggregately, collectively, collaboratively, that is the Experiencing of Divinity at the level of Completion.

Completion is achieved by each aspect of Divinity achieving *its particular expression* in fullness.

Divinity empowers Divinity to produce this result. That is to say, Life empowers Life to produce more Life, and to express Life in fullness— because the Expression of Life in Fullness is Divinity's Desire.

That is your desire, too.

From the earliest days of your infancy to the breath you took a moment ago, that has been your yearning, your dream, and your goal. And now that you remember this, it seems obvious to you. It seems obvious, too, that there is no *difference* between your innermost yearning and the desire of God.

God's desire is implanted in your Soul, which is the aspect of your being that is the Essential Essence, the part of you that carries the Divine Impulse throughout this lifetime. (And, indeed, through all lifetimes.)

The Soul is also the aspect of you that remembers this. It never forgets, it cannot forget, because it *is* The Memory Itself. And so, the Soul is constantly Aware of All There Is To Know, throughout Eternity. Your Mind, on the other hand, is simply a storehouse of present life Experiences.

> A *Soul Knowing:*
> Completion is achieved by each aspect of Divinity achieving its particular expression in fullness.

(All of this has been explained before in separate parts of this exploration, we know. It is being brought together now in a way that hopefully allows the final puzzle piece to fit.)

If What One Desires is known by the Soul, and if what your experience tells you that *you* should desire is held in the Mind, then the challenge and the invitation of Life is to bring the two together, with the Soul informing the Mind, expanding the Mind, enlarging the database of the Mind, so that the mechanics of Reality Creation produce a new and grander experience of Who You Are.

This is the Special Invitation you are receiving in this moment. You are being invited to allow *What One Desires* to become *your* desire, *consciously.*

You are being invited to turn what you know conceptually into what you experience functionally.

A way to do this is to make *What One Desires* your new mantra, so that each time your Mind is confronted with any exterior perplexing circumstance or event and seeks to formulate a response, you call upon your Self to remember not what the Mind alone wants, but what the Soul and the Mind together urge, so that the Totality of You can choose to express and experience *What One Desires.*

This is but another way of declaring: "Not my will, but Thine."

20

What The Path of the Soul Is Not

LET'S BE CLEAR ABOUT SOMETHING before we go on, before we describe what it means to focus your life on What One Desires by following The Path of the Soul.

People do not leave The Path of the Soul because they do not want to stay on the path; they leave The Path because they don't know what The Path looks like.

People get off The Path by mistake, not by intention. They would rather stay than stray, but they stray from The Path nonetheless, because some of the tracks away from The Path have been taken by so many, and are so well-worn, that *they look like The Path.*

The pursuit of love looks like The Path.

The pursuit of security looks like The Path.

The pursuit of success looks like The Path.

The pursuit of power looks like The Path.

The pursuit of money looks like The Path.

The pursuit of happiness looks like The Path.

The pursuit of sex looks like The Path.

The pursuit of popularity looks like The Path.

The pursuit of peace looks like The Path.

The pursuit of social justice looks like The Path.

None of these trails are The Path, but all of these can look, from time to time, *exactly like The Path,* appearing to be the walkway that will take you where you want to go—especially if you aren't entirely *clear* about where you want to go (much less the fastest way to get there).

If the first step toward the actual path is what you believe about God, the purpose of your Life, and about your Soul, the second step is moving into clarity about where you want to go. You have to want to go where the Soul is going, and not where the Body or the Mind sometimes wish to go—or think they *should* be going.

The Soul is going to a place called Completion, and that goal can be reached on a moment-to-moment basis, step-by-step, stage-by-stage, in one's life.

If you've jumped ahead to this Conversation without reading all of Part Two, you have missed the deeper explanation of that. You may think, then, that Life is about some longer-range goal. Or some loftier aspiration. Or about some more particular or more easily articulated and generally agreed-with outcomes, such as those listed above.

You can be excused for holding such notions, because some of these, at least, are exceedingly worthwhile objectives. Who can argue with the creating of Love, Peace, or Social Justice as the goal of one's life?

Only if we are spiritually awakened—or if we have spent a lifetime working for those other things and, having achieved those goals at least in part, found that *this is not it,* and we are still not fulfilled—could we know that the Path of the Soul must be going *somewhere else.*

> *A Soul Knowing:*
> Taking the Path of the Soul will change everything.

Further, only if we *take* the Path of the Soul to that Somewhere Else Place could we know that *in* that place will be found all the things we were looking for and struggling to create by *leaving* The Path—including everything on the list above.

You can, as was said earlier here, trust that if the whole of humanity paid attention to the Soul's Agenda and to what it takes to complete it, the items on the above list, and the many other things that all humans hope for, would then "show up" in our world automatically. It is already occurring that way in individual lives all over the planet.

So what does it "look like" to take the Path of the Soul, to express and experience What One Desires?

It will change everything.

It will change how you think, how you feel, how you speak, how you act, how you *inter*act, how you love, how you work, how you play, how you eat, and yes, even how you sleep.

You will sleep better than you have ever slept before, because your Mind will be more rested than it has ever been before, because your Heart will be more open than it has ever been before, because your Soul will be more heard than it has ever been before.

You will still do many of the same things you did before, but you will do them for a different reason, in a different way, with a different purpose, seeking a different outcome, and producing a different result.

You will suddenly seem very clear about the "why" behind every "what" that is occurring in your life, and when you are clear about the "why" you will intuitively know "what" to do about "what" is occurring— and it will not "occur" to you to do anything else.

"Doingness" will not be absent from your life, but it will henceforth be a reflection, a demonstration, and an announcement of where you are, rather than an attempt to get somewhere.

Abruptly, everything will seem perfectly "okay" in your life just the way everything *is*—even if yesterday you would have called the way things are "not okay."

You will feel this sudden shift not because you will have become apathetic about the way things are, but precisely the opposite—because you have become fully *responsive* to how things are. You will be *fully* responding—that is, from The Totality of You; from your Body, your Mind, *and your Soul*, rather than from your Body and your Mind alone, which is how most people on Earth have been responding to most occurrences most of the time. Which, in *turn*, is why 98% of the people have spent 98% of their time on things that don't matter.

21

A Look At What One Desires and What One Does on The Path

WHILE THE WAY to *know* What One Desires is to bring your Soul into your Mind, combining the two into One, the way to *express What One Desires* is to then bring the Body into this process. This is called Integration. It brings the Whole of You into Integrity. Now the Holy Trinity is completely realized—made *real*—in you. This is what spiritual mastery is all about.

When, in any Moment, the *three* aspects of The Totality of You are fully integrated, in that Moment The Only Thing That Matters is *What One Desires.*

You have reached Completion.

You have Mastered The Moment.

What One Desires manifests through you, in you, as you. The Body, the Mind, and the Soul out-picture in the Physical Realm that which is known in the Spiritual Realm. Divinity is then *experienced.* And this experience is created through what you are *being*—not through what you are doing.

Each time you are Being Love fully, you have taken the Path of the Soul and you have achieved Completion. You are there. You have arrived. You have reached your destination.

Each time you are Being Understanding fully, you have taken the Path of the Soul and you have achieved Completion. You are there. You have arrived. You have reached your destination.

Each time you are Being Compassion fully, you have taken the Path of the Soul and you have achieved Completion. You are there. You have arrived. You have reached your destination.

Each time—in every *nanosecond*—that you are demonstrating Patience, Caring, Tenderness, Clarity, Kindness, Wisdom, Generosity, Acceptance, Goodness, or Charity *fully,* you have taken the Path of the Soul and you have achieved Completion. You are there. You have arrived. You have reached your destination.

> *A Soul Knowing:*
> You are proceeding
> to the next stage
> in your spiritual
> evolution.

If there is a moment when you are demonstrating all of these things simultaneously, you have, in that moment, in that nanosecond, no farther to go. You have expressed, and thus experienced, Divinity at the highest level of which your present level of Consciousness is capable.

The exciting thing is, your level of Consciousness will then immediately expand, allowing you to move farther into grander and grander experiences.

This is precisely what is happening right now. This is exactly what is occurring *as you are reading this book,* and during these very days and times in your life. You have achieved all of these things one by one, and yes, you have even achieved these things simultaneously, already in your life. Now you are going to the next level. Now you are proceeding to the next stage in your spiritual evolution.

~

Since you so easily remember all of this now, the question becomes: Why don't you remember it at the moment when you are stepping to the next stage and could *use* these reminders—in the nanosecond when your choice to demonstrate and personify these aspects of Divinity at the next highest level could alter a moment dramatically and change your life (not to mention the life of another)?

As it is, there are still moments in your life when you do *not* feel loving, understanding, compassionate, patient, caring, tender, clear, kind, wise, generous, accepting, good, or charitable. *Why not?* Especially when you *know* that this is the way you *would* feel if you were your Highest Self.

Why can't you rise to that level more often? At will? And stay there?

It could be because in some of the Moments when Life conditions are inviting you to absorb more of the Awareness of your Soul, your "sponge" is full, cannot soak up any more of the "ocean," and simply needs to be rung out.

In such Moments your Mind loses touch with your Soul, forgets some of what the Soul knows, and imagines that you are being attacked, or are about to be, and must defend yourself, because it imagines that your first priority is to survive.

Or it could be that your Mind believes that you are about to lose something, or have already lost it, or are being denied something, or have never had it, or are being made wrong about something, or are losing control of something (if not everything).

Or it could be that you feel you just don't have the time and energy right now to keep plugging away, keep plowing ahead, your face constantly to the wind. Maybe you'd just like the wind at your back for a while. For just a few blessed moments, thank you very much . . .

~

What you need are tools. Devices. Methods or approaches that could *place* the wind at your back, that could *give* you smooth sailing for a while, that could *clear* The Path for at least a little bit, the part just ahead, so that every . . . single . . . step did not have to be a Major Struggle, requiring a Major Effort.

Well, you've come to the right place. You've brought yourself to the right place. You *created* this place, through you own willingness to be here. You demonstrated that willingness the moment you picked up this book. And . . .

. . . it goes deeper than that . . .

22

Who Are You and Who Am I?

My Dear Soul Friend . . . Are you beginning to see what is going on here?

It is your deep desire to call forth *your own* wisdom, *your own* awareness of how to solve "the unavoidable, intractable, and oppressive problems of everyday life (pocketbook issues, work stresses, relationships, etc. . . .)," that is projecting that wisdom and awareness outward into your exterior world, just as it always has, causing your own inner knowing to "show up" as a book or a movie or a lecture. Or the chance utterance of a friend on the street. Or the lyrics of the next song you hear on the radio.

These little incidents in life are co-created by you and many other Souls. That is why they are called *"co . . . incidents."*

You are constantly co-creating your reality with the Rest Of You. You begin to understand this as you begin to remember that We Are All One, and that the other people on the earth are simply the Rest Of You.

Moving from the *Knowing* to the *Experiencing* of this is the Ultimate Expression of Completion. It is when you have experienced your Self fully not only as *one* of the aspects of Divinity (love, compassion, understanding, patience, acceptance, etc.), but as *every* aspect in every one of Its endless manifestations. It is when you experience All of Oneness All at Once.

It is at this Moment that you can identify with both the "victim" and the "perpetrator," with both the person wearing the white garment and the dark garment—knowing that you, yourself, have worn both at one time or another, and that you love and forgive yourself still, because you know that confusion is not a crime, and that villainy in any form is all a form of simple forgetting.

Such holding of the Total Awareness of the Soul in the Total Comprehension of the Mind is more normal and more usual than you think. Again, the trick is to *keep* it there.

> A Soul Knowing:
> Your Soul holds a
> complete awareness
> of Ultimate Reality.

Now . . . have you not ever noticed how often it is that just when your Mind seeks to regain its Total Comprehension—when the need for an answer to some particular life dilemma becomes most acute—the Right and Perfect Answer often spontaneously pops up right in front of your face, as part of life itself, from a seemingly "separate" source?

Yet what if *there is no such thing as a Separate Source?* What if there is only One Source—and that Source lies with you? What if it sometimes manifests *outside* of you, but it *originates* within you?

Can you conceive of such a thing?

~

Okay, so let's talk about this Single Source that lies within all of us.

In some conceptualizations—including the messages of *Conversations with God* (CWG) that inform this text—it is called the Soul.

CWG says that your Soul holds a complete Awareness of Ultimate Reality. That is, it knows whence it came, where it is now, and that to which it shall return.

It is from this vast Awareness that your Soul retrieves the data and co-creates, with other souls, the conditions, situations, and circumstances arising before you in just the right way at just the right time in your life. (Even as it is doing right now.)

Indeed, this is the Soul's *job*. This is the Soul's *purpose* and *function*.

Many people have lived their whole lives without hearing that. Perhaps you are one of them. If you are, all of your life you've heard about the soul, the Soul, the *Soul,* but no one could ever tell you *why you had one.* Many people may have told you *that* you had one, but no one told you *why* you had one.

Now you know why; you remember your Soul's purpose and function. But be careful! If you are not careful, it could look as if this *book* just told you that, when in fact *your own Soul* just told you that.

~

Are you seeing how this all works? Your Soul called this forth, bringing it *before* you from *within* you—even as your Mind will insist on imagining that it is coming from somewhere outside of you.

Your Soul will continue to use all sorts of methods and approaches—even those that *bypass* your Mind (indeed, especially those) in order to *rouse* your Mind, thus to educate your Mind about how to meet the challenges and overcome the obstacles of day-to-day Life.

It will also use tools and devices that appear to be totally *separate* from the Mind—such as a book that you "just happened" to pick up. In this way it will appear to the Mind that one has "found the answer elsewhere."

In the beginning of one's life quest for greater truth, when one is a Seeker, this often makes the answer more acceptable, because not many people are ready at this early stage to embrace the notion that they had the answer all along.

You, however, are no longer at the beginning of your quest. You are hardly an Early Stage Seeker. You are now a Serious Student, or you wouldn't be reading this. So you are very ready now to dance with the idea that all the Awareness you will ever need to solve all the problems you will ever have is, and has always been, within you—and that you are simply *calling it forth* from time to time, using a variety of methods and devices, some of which have made it *appear* as though the Awareness you are seeking is being found outside of you.

To others, looking on from the sidelines of your life, it may very well seem this way. You've no doubt often told your family and your friends, "I've just read the greatest book!" or "I've just seen a fabulous movie!" or "I've just heard a marvelous lecture!"—and then, when they see some change in you, they naturally assume that the book, the movie, or the lecture is the source of your new Awareness.

Nothing could be further from the truth.

23

A Dare, from the Author to the Author

OKAY, NOW COMES THE MIND-BOGGLING PART. This entire book has been a wide-ranging exploration, but right now you're going to be invited to undertake one of the most unusual explorations of all. You're going to be invited to explore not just the idea, but the *experience* that there is only One of us—and therefore, no separation between you and the author of this book.

The "rational" side of your "mystical" side (yes, the two can exist simultaneously) may fairly easily have accepted this book's basic notion that "remembering and experiencing all of the insights here this is why you came to this moment," as well as the idea that "*you* have called forth this wisdom and this understanding," but now, exactly where are we going . . . ?

You've just been reminded that *What One Desires* is The Only Thing That Matters . . . and so, now where are we going?

We are going to a place of Mind where you may know experientially one's greatest desire: no separation from anyone or anything; the end of loneliness forever.

~

As you take this next courageous step in your self-exploration, we want to suggest that you begin with questions that may have occurred to you earlier:

"How can I claim to have called forth *my* wisdom by reading someone *else's* book? Is this not what I have always done—looked to someone else for answers?"

The response offered here: Perhaps it is what you have seemed to have done in the past, but it is not what you are clear that you are doing now. This is different. Now, in this moment, you are Aware that when you actively call forth wisdom from within, it "shows up" in a hundred different ways across a thousand moments:

The lyrics to the next song you hear on the radio.

The message splashed across the billboard on the next highway you travel.

The chance utterance in the next conversation you overhear, or of a friend you "just happen" to run into on the street.

And yes, even "you," seemingly talking to yourself.

Which brings us back to this book—and the statements that led off Chapter 4. It can "look like" the wisdom on these pages is coming from somewhere else, but it is *you* who have *called it forth*.

You will remember that in Chapter 3 it was said that you can call forth wisdom in two ways: One way is to gather it from a place that appears to be outside of you. That is what you appear to be doing right now. A second way is to gather information from a place that is *inside* of you. That is what you are *actually* doing right now.

It *looks like* you are doing the first, but you are actually doing the second.

Now, as you delve even more deeply into the wisdom that you have brought forward, you might ask yourself: Is this a book that I "just happened" to be drawn to, and that I "just happen" to now be reading? Do I really think that this is all "just happening"—or could it be the reverse: that it is all happening justly?

Might it be occurring in just the right way, at just the right time, for just the right reason, just perfectly?

To take this all to new territory, could it be that you not only "found" this book so easily, but that you found it so easy to read, because this really is all just *you* calling to yourself and talking to yourself?

Just for this moment, let's pretend that it is.

Just for the experiment of it, just for *the mental exercise of it . . .* pretend that what you are holding in your hands is a book written *for* you *by* you, called forth through what appears to be Another . . . but who may not be "another" at all.

Again, there's a reason for this experiment, and it has to do with bringing you a direct experience of The Only Thing That Matters. So, will you "play"? Begin the fun by assuming that you created and brought to yourself every Soul Knowing you have here "remembered," simply using an exterior device to do so.

"Well, if that's the case, then this book might just as well be written in the First Person, as if it were *not* written by someone else at all," you might say. And indeed, it might as well be.

So now you are invited by Life Itself to imagine in this moment that the author of this book is you—that you are *writing to yourself*.

You realize now that you were told earlier in very clear terms that Life's Invitation is to now engage you in the process of exploring with *yourself* many things. This moment in your life is all about turning inward, looking at what you already know, but that you may simply not have been remembering.

So why not create a real "switch" right now? Why not entertain a most unusual notion? Why not change the Narrative Voice of this book from the Third Person to the First Person?

Will you dare to put this book into your own voice—to read it as if it truly *were* your own lost diary?

24

Taking the Dare

Actually, I like this idea. I can easily imagine that this book is being written *to* me *from* me, *for* me *by* me. I like the idea that the "me" who I Am is much bigger than the one physical form that currently calls itself Me.

I have often experienced "talking to myself," or "thinking out loud," and so allowing myself to consider that this book is a *written version of that experience* is an easy transition.

I can imagine that these thoughts and words are simply being transcribed for me by the Part of Me whom others refer to by a different name and think of as the author of this book.

To people who do not understand what I am allowing myself to experiment with and experience right now, this may all seem a little strange. For them it will absolutely be true that someone else has written this book, and that I am merely reading it.

If I were to share with them what I'm experiencing in this moment by suddenly switching my point of view from that of the Reader to that of the Writer—if I were to tell them that I truly believe it is very possible that I am at the very least a Collaborative Cause of this writing, and so, in that sense, that I am The Source of It—they would surely say that I've just lost touch with reality.

There's a certain irony in that, because it feels as though I have just now gotten *in touch* with Reality. Reality with a capital 'R.'

Again.

At last.

It's true . . . I *do* know all that I am encountering here. I *do* know that the "someone else" who has written this book is merely Another Part of Me.

I've always understood that all of *life* is just Another Part of Me. And so I know now that I *called forth* this book—that I am calling it forth now, in real time—as yet one more way to remind my Self of the largest truths of my life.

I know that the Oneness of All of Humanity (and of the entire Universe, really) is a difficult concept for many people to embrace. They are not familiar yet with M Theory, which today's physicists are advancing to offer, finally, a Theory of Everything, and which supplies mathematical evidence for the notion that we do not live in a Universe at all, but a Multiverse, made up of *an infinite number* of universes—all created and connected by a single phenomenon called The Membrane.

People do not know that this is not "New Age nonsense," but today's new *science*.

This notion that I am One with the Author, that the Author is One with me, and that all of us on this planet are One With Each Other, seems very UNscientific, running counter to everything we've been told by our cultures, our clans, our families, our communities, and our religions, and calling up the opposite of everything we see reflected in our politics, our economics, our societies, and, in fact, our entire world from top to bottom.

That does not make it any less true.

My invitation from Life is to "judge not by appearances," but to hold to the Truth. This Truth will allow me to see others, and to *treat* others, as aspects of myself.

That alone could change my life.

If I did nothing else, seeing others and treating others as aspects of myself would alter everything in my experience.

But that isn't enough. Not anymore. I'm tired of settling for small steps or simple aphorisms. It is time now to enter into deep, honest, self-examination. That's part of the reason I came to this book; that is part of the purpose of writing this to myself. I need to ask myself some questions. Some important, even pointed, questions:

Does it feel as though what I'm doing these days is what an evolved being would do? Beyond the issue of *survival,* beyond "taking care of business" or slogging through the day "doing what needs to be done," how much of what I'm "up to" feels like what really matters, and how much feels like just "stuff and nonsense"—or, in Shakespeare's words, *Much Ado About Nothing . . . ?*

Are my minutes fulfilling? Are my hours ringing with satisfaction? Are my days overflowing with contentment? Are my weeks and months teeming with accomplishment of my Soul's agenda?

Are my years brimming with spiritual radiance and soulful, Divine expression and experience? Or do I awaken on milestone days—birthdays, anniversaries, times of celebration—with a vague feeling of how fast time is passing and how slowly I have progressed at what I came here to accomplish—and how difficult it is to accomplish it . . . ?

For that matter, have I always been clear that there *is* something specific that I came here to accomplish? If so, have I known exactly what that is?

I guess I should not be surprised or embarrassed if I have not. It turns out that 98% of the world's people do not. And it's not their fault. And it's not my fault if I find myself even now, at least from time to time, among them. Because nobody told them, and nobody told *me,* what really matters.

Oh, they've tried to tell us. Some people have tried to convince us. And many, many of us listened to those peoeple, because to know something for *certain*—as religions and politics allow us to think that we do—feels better than to not know.

But the more *I* listened the more I knew that what others were "buying into" of what still others were telling *them* couldn't possibly be true.

So I moved away from all of their agendas. I may not have known where I was *going*, but I knew what I wanted to get *away* from.

The result is that I am spending less time these days in that larger group. And right now I am not even in it . . . or I would never have this book in my hand. It is wonderful that I am not among that 98% now, and that I spend less and less time there, because there's nothing worse than spending most of one's life on things that just simply don't matter.

No, wait, yes there is. It would be worse to *not know* what *does* matter. It would be worse to not know that what I am doing here is taking a Sacred Journey, fulfilling a Divine Purpose.

~

Well, I don't have to worry about that. I understand now—and I understand that I've *understood* what I understand for quite a while. I simply wasn't doing very much about it.

Oh, I dabbled now and then. I read some things, went to some events, made some promises to myself. But, truth be told, I didn't jump *into* it whole hog. I was a "chicken" about it.

One day the Chicken and the Pig were walking down the road when they came upon a huge billboard. On it was a picture of a plate of ham and eggs. Above the picture was the headline: The World's Favorite Breakfast.

The Chicken turned to the Pig with the biggest smile. "Look at that!" she said. "Doesn't that make you proud?"

"That's easy for you to say," replied the Pig. "For you it's partial dedication. For me it's total commitment."

~

I think I'm ready for total commitment. I've had enough of shaking my head in dismay and feeling sadness in my heart each time I see the news on my computer or turn on the television or glimpse the headline of an evening paper.

More and more, the world in which I live feels like a world to which I don't belong. I feel strangely out of place, as if someone dropped me off somewhere in the cosmos where the local inhabitants act very strange and I don't know why they're doing what they're doing, because it all seems so *opposite* to what a normal, loving, caring, intelligent being would do . . .

I am done with this, and I'm so glad I came here—brought myself here—because I've wanted it explained, before I move forward, why things are the way they are, and what I can do to get back to what matters.

So I've made my decision. I'm on board. I'm *going for it.*

Can my decision be experienced *totally* while I am in my present physical human form? No. It cannot. One physical lifetime is too limited for the Unlimited Oneness to fit into. I get that. Does my True Identity *have* to be experienced *totally* for my life to have meaning and to be fulfilling? No. I get that, too. I am clear now that attaining even portions or aspects of the Divine (Oneness being the sum of those aspects) is sufficient for me to know immense joy and fulfillment.

I am also clear that sticking to the Agenda of the Soul is just the challenge I have been preparing for all these years as I now move into the extraordinary times just ahead.

The whole Earth is moving through these important moments with me even now, and I want to help *create* those moments, not merely witness them. I remember now that I can best do that by focusing much more of my life on The Only Thing That Matters.

Yet how can *What One Desires* produce good for oneself and for the world—and what does a clear focus on *What One Desires* "look like" in Life's on-the-ground, day-to-day moments?

That is the next great question. And, by going within, I am certain that I can find many answers being drawn *to* me, *by* me. One way might be for me to *continue with this book*—but as the Writer, or the Reader?

25

A Demonstration of Free Will

THE PROBLEM Is that I seem to move in and out of the level of "knowing" that I am experiencing now. I seem to "get there," then I find myself "not there"—sometimes in the very next Moment . . . just as described at the end of Part Two of this book.

Right now I'm "there" again. I understand the point the book is making that We Are All One, and that, therefore, what I do for me I do for others, and that what I do for others I do for me. And so, focusing on *What One Desires* is not "selfish" at all.

I also understand what this text is telling me when it declares that the writer and the reader are, at the level of Essence, in no way separate—and that I am at choice, always, about whether I choose to experience that.

And here is something else that I know: I know that the Illusion of Separation sometimes serves humanity. In fact, if it *didn't* serve the species, I have to believe that we would have eliminated the Illusion altogether a long time ago. Evolution itself would surely have produced that result. But we've kept this Illusion of Separation in place because we see that it in many ways serves us.

Now it seems to me that what would be most beneficial to us at this stage of our development as an evolving species would be to step aside from the Separation Illusion where it serves us to do so (if it could more rapidly end global suffering, for instance, or create a larger and more joyful experience of the Self), and to continue to *use* the Illusion when it facilitates our growth or understanding. As, for instance, when the Illusion makes it possible for the human Mind to take in, much more readily, true wisdom and deep insight.

In my own case, for example, I find that if I hold the idea that *I* am writing this book (as opposed to simply seeing myself reading the words of another), the words seem to have less weight somehow. I give them less credence or credibility.

For reasons not entirely clear to me (but probably having to do with my own spiritual immaturity and a resulting refusal to see myself as my own spiritual "authority"), I feel much more "open" to huge insights about Life when I experience that they are coming from a Source Outside Myself.

I feel certain this is not the same for everyone (I don't sense that Parahamansa Yogananda second-guessed himself very much in *Autobiography of a Yogi,* for instance), but as the person holding this book right now, I find it easier to "hear" what it has to say when I don't imagine that I am writing the book myself.

And do you know what? The thought just struck me that *perhaps this is why we have placed God outside of ourselves.*

So this little "thought experiment" was very interesting, and it did give me the direct experience that both the Wisdom brought to me here and the Wisdom residing within myself are One and The Same—but, since the ongoing experience of Oneness is not mandatory (as the writing here itself points out), I'm pretty much ready to step back into the profile of the reader, stepping aside from any idea that I am the author, if only so that by creating a greater distance between the Thinker and the Thought, I can embrace the Thought Itself more fully.

So . . . I shall herewith return to the profile of the Reader—even if in truth the Author and I *are* One—as my latest demonstration of Free Will in determining how I choose to experience Life.

26

It Is Time for the Struggle to Be Over

BRAVO! EXCELLENT! What a wonderful—and unusual—experience, yes? You won't find *that* happening very often in books. We (you and I) used this unconventional (if not *outlandish*) device to graphically and vividly demonstrate how a simple change in your point of view about anything can dramatically alter your experience.

When you see things differently, when you bring in the Awareness of Soul as your Mind encounters the data brought to you by your Body, your entire perspective changes. And your perspective, of course, creates your perception. And your perception creates your beliefs. And your beliefs create your behaviors. And your behaviors produce your experience.

Bringing you the Awareness of your Soul to dramatically alter your experience is what this book is all about! So now, let's see if we might alter your experience around "struggle" and "suffering" . . .

~

Dear One . . .

It has not been easy, this journey you are on. It has required courage and determination, patience and understanding, a willingness to keep going against all odds, a commitment to continually seek the light even as the darkness grows, and to reach for the good when everything *but* the good seems to be all around you.

It has asked so much of you, this journey—and you have given what has been asked.

God bless you, *you have given what has been asked.*

Now it is time for your struggle to be over. You deserve that. You've earned that.

Your Soul knows this, of course, and agrees. That is why you wound up being drawn to these words. You are going to be given here a most powerful tool—perhaps the most powerful ever created—for bringing an end to struggling and suffering in your life.

Let's take a look at it, opening with a glimpse at the nature and the cause of struggle and suffering itself.

When you have reached one of many moments of Completion of The Sacred Journey—which, as has now been explained, can occur in any one of the Moments in a lifetime—your immediate wish will be to experience *more* of that, in even greater form. And so your Soul will begin the whole process all over again—yet not starting from the beginning. Rather, starting from right where you are now.

> *A Soul Knowing:*
> Completion of the
> Sacred Journey can
> occur at any Moment.

In a sense, you will be born again, having Completed your Sacred Journey. Now you will undertake the Journey again, with a new Destination, with the goal pushed a little farther out.

Now you might think that this will be a source of frustration, and it may have been in your past, but it will be no longer, because now you know what's going on. (That's why you brought yourself here, in fact. To end the frustration. That's why you have just reminded yourself of The Only Thing That Matters.)

When you have become fully aware, *you will never want the process that has been described here to end.* The bliss of evolving to higher and higher levels of Divinity will become Life's ultimate attraction, and a natural reaction. It is exactly that: a "reaction"—or, if you please, a re-action—in the sense that you are *acting again* as Who You Really Are. It is a recognizing—that is, a re-*cognizing,* or a knowing again—of your True Identity. It is the fundamental attraction of Life to More Life. It is the attraction of God to God Itself. It is the Impulse of the Divine, in You.

This is the "Law of Attraction"—not the power to magnetize cars, jewels, and bicycles.

～

The Sacred Journey as it is expressed in physical terms is sometimes called Evolution. In metaphysical terms it could be described as a process in which one's destination is one's embarkation. The End becomes The Beginning in the Circle of God.

When the clock strikes Midnight, what has happened? Has the day just ended, or has a new day just begun? And when, exactly, has the first happened, and when has the second? *Or is it possible that both are happening at once?*

This is what is true on The Path of the Soul. The path appears to be a *circle.* Yet you do not experience yourself "going around in circles," as in "getting nowhere." Rather, you experience your Self spiraling upward.

Think of a *Slinky,* the children's toy that looks for all the world like a one-dimensional circle when viewed from directly above or below, but which reveals itself to be one continuous multidimensional element that stretches into a spiral, using its own momentum for energy.

Ironically, this description of a children's toy could also be a description of the path taken by the Totality of You (TOY). This is the *real* Toy Story.

～

Now please know that it is understood by the Universe that even as you read this you're moving through a new stage in your own personal, spiritual, and emotional development. So it is important at this vulnerable time that you not be discouraged. This point was made earlier, and it is worth repeating.

It was promised that you would be given a tool that would help you to *not* be discouraged, a tool that would eliminate struggle and suffering from your life. We're about to give you that tool here. But first, we need to place what is going to be said here into context.

Let it be acknowledged that there have been sad and difficult experiences that many people have undergone in their lives, and that many are continuing to face today, and that these events and their impact are very real. What is written here is not meant to in any way minimalize or marginalize that reality, nor the ordeals that many people are going through.

To the unaware observer the challenging events in the lives of millions may seem like a cruel way for what has here been called the "Divine Purpose" to be fulfilled.

Why should people have to suffer in order to demonstrate to themselves, to others, or to God, Who They Really Are—or to provide God with the experience of Divinity?

That is an appropriate, obvious, and important question. It commands our attention, as rightly it should. Every thinking person must receive a satisfactory answer to that question if the spiritual concepts in this text are to have a shred of credibility, a leg to stand on.

The answer to this question was also part of an earlier narrative, and also deserves to be repeated here:

People do not have to suffer in order to express and experience Who They Really Are. This is neither God's request nor God's demand.

This does not mean, however, that there will not be sadness and pain in people's lives. There will be. There is, and there will be. Yet there is a blessed reason for sadness and pain, and tears are not signs of suffering, but of *release* from suffering.

Tears wash away our Illusions, bringing us to the calm place where Divine Reality Resides.

What is going to shared here now is not said lightly. It would be a mistake to presume that deep understandings such as that offered in the following paragraphs are presented off-handedly or blithely.

Just the opposite is true. They are presented seriously, and are meant to be taken seriously. They are offered from a place of full honoring of those who have suffered, and from a space of hoping to help those who are still suffering now, to bring their suffering and their struggling to an end.

From this gentle place we wish to observe that sadness, pain, and suffering are not all the same thing.

Now this does not mean that we should ignore all suffering, look past all of another's torment, and proceed as if nothing bad is happening in the world. Quite the contrary. All of the circumstances on our planet, all of the conditions of Life, are placed *before* us *by* us (remember always: we are acting *co-jointly*; there is only One of us) in order that we may decide, express, and experience who we really are in relationship to them.

> *A Soul Knowing:*
> Sadness, pain, and suffering are not all the same thing.

Thus do those who suffer, and those who end the suffering of others, both experience Who We All Really Are. And This is exactly what is happening upon the earth. Everything that is happening is happening perfectly so that all may awaken.

Many Souls choose to be instruments of our awakening, and so are enduring enormous challenges, with many even dying, in order that all of us may awaken within us the Divine qualities of compassion, caring, understanding, patience, love, and, most of all, the Unity and Oneness of Life. Witnessing this, all of us of course experience deep sadness. At the deepest level, we are sad that *this is what it takes* for us to awaken. Yet this does not mean that suffering is required.

~

Sadness is emotional evidence of your deep humanity. If you did not love, if you did not care, if you did not feel deep compassion, you would be truly sad about very little. Sadness is a badge of honor. Wear it proudly. You have earned it with the wounds of your heart.

Pain is a psychological or physiological response to exterior stimuli. The fact that you experience it is evidence of the generosity of your Soul in taking on the human condition. When you bear it with courage and with strength, you demonstrate the nobility of your Sacred Journey.

Suffering is the Mind's *response* to sadness or pain. If you suffer while experiencing sadness or pain, you have clearly made a decision that *you should not now be experiencing it.* It is this decision, not the sadness or pain itself, that is the cause of your suffering.

Sadness and physical or emotional pain is what's arising. Suffering is your announcement that you may not fully understand *why* it is arising, and how it all fits into the Agenda of the Soul.

When you fully comprehend exactly what is taking place in your life, as well as the Process of Life Itself, then your suffering ends, even if the pain continues. *Nothing changes, but everything is different.*

> A Soul Knowing:
> A way has been found for the Sacred Journey to continue, yet for the struggle and suffering to end.

The biggest difference is that you no longer feel that you are the victim in any life situation. And with the end of victimization comes the end of struggle and suffering.

There even come times in the experience of many when one's struggle and pain can actually be *celebrated* (believe it or not), even as it is being experienced, changing its very definition from suffering to joy.

Anyone who has had an aching tooth pulled and endured the endless machinations of the dentist and the unpleasant injection of Novocain knows exactly what this is about.

More profoundly, anyone who has experienced the pain of the death of a loved one, all the while knowing that their dear one's next experience is a gloriously happy reuniting with all whom they have ever loved, and with Divinity Itself, knows exactly what this is all about.

And any woman who has given birth to a long-awaited and cherished child knows exactly what a pain that turns to joy—even as the pain is experienced—is all about.

It is when you make this shift with regard to *everything in your life* that you switch from suffering to joy in the expressions and experiences of your life. From then on, *nothing* can touch you in a way that causes you abject suffering—even though you will *not* be immune to sadness or pain.

~

The question, then, is: How do you make this shift regarding everything in your life? How can you transform suffering into joy, and struggle into peace?

Mystics and masters through the ages have assured us that we can do this. A way *has* been found for the Sacred Journey to continue, yet for the struggle and suffering to end.

Life has given us a remarkably powerful tool that makes this possible. But now, this warning: When you hear of it, it may sound simplistic and overrated.

Do not be fooled.

It can change everything.

The tool?

GRATITUDE.

27

An Enormous Power Has Just Been Placed in Your Hands

Now you have one missing piece of the puzzle. Now you have one transformative tool. (You will be given others here as well.) It is a device with immense power—a simple device that can transform almost any moment, almost miraculously, almost immediately.

But let's not get ahead of ourselves. Let's understand exactly what this tool is.

Gratitude is not merely an emotion, it is a decision.

So powerful is this decision that it becomes a definition and a declaration. It defines and declares your experience of Here and Now. And hence, your reality.

Gratitude can be a simple emotional reaction, or it can be a magnificent spiritual creation. It is a simple reaction when your Mind is on Automatic. It is a magnificent creation when your Mind has merged with your Soul in making a combined choice about any Present Moment.

In every Moment of your life your choice is always the same: to move into Reaction or Creation.

(You might have a little fun noticing that "reaction" and "creation" are very close to being the same word. Only the C and the R need to be reversed. When you C what you have always been meant to C, then you R what you always R—and the course of your *life* is reversed.)

∼

While Gratitude may be one of the most powerful tools your Mind has ever been given, it may also be the most underutilized. This is no doubt because most people are not aware of the immense power of Gratitude to reverse a thought that is at the foundation of all suffering.

As earlier noted, the central cause of suffering is the idea that *something is happening that should not be happening*. Gratitude unleashes an energy that turns this idea on its head, announcing that just because something is unpleasant does not mean it is unbidden, unwelcome, or unwanted.

We have already demonstrated that pain (both physical and emotional) can, in *fact*, be bidden, welcome, and wanted—for any one of a number of reasons. Yet if the Mind *thinks* that a particular pain is "unwanted," it will not abide it—and that is precisely what creates struggle in one's life, and suffering.

> *A Soul Knowing:*
> Gratitude is not a tool with which to fool the Mind, it is a tool with which to open the Mind.

Struggle is the result of the Mind rejecting what the Soul offers. It is the Mind deciding to go off in another direction, veering from the Path of the Soul. Suffering is the emotional product of that decision. Both struggle and suffering are creations of the Mind, which is where your reality is created.

What your Mind *thinks* about something is crucial in determining how you experience it—and Gratitude can cause you to change your Mind.

Yet Gratitude is not a tool with which to fool the Mind; it is a tool with which to open the Mind. It expands your normal, limited thinking to include a counterintuitive truth: that even when something seems "bad" for you, it can actually be good for you.

∼

Underneath this truth lies a deeper one: Nothing that *ever* happens is "bad" for you, or it wouldn't be happening. Life is incapable of producing an event or condition that does not carry you to the next place in your evolution, and that is not designed for your next expression of Divinity. Since the expression of Divinity is the reason you are here, you can be sure that everything that is placed before you *appears* before you to serve this Divine Purpose. (In other words, *your* purpose.)

And so we say, *Thank you, God.* We give thanks for the opportunity to heal an old injury, to close an old wound, to alter an old pattern, to shift an old reality, to release an old story, to change an old idea, and to create a new experience of Self and Life.

~

Okay. That's saying a lot. And you might now ask, "How is all this possible? How can all that healing and change occur?"

To see this clearly you must observe, with Gratitude, Life's most wonderful gift:

RELIABLE REPETITION

To explain: You can depend on Life to be repetitious. Very few events or situations arising in your life will be much of a surprise to you anymore. Not in the sense of your never having experienced anything like them before. How you are going to react, then, can actually be anticipated by you, and you can reject your prior decisions about such events or situations if you wish.

And *that* is Life's great secret. The greatest secret is not the Law of Attraction, but the *Law of Retraction*.

This is a tool used to *retract* old decisions and make new ones, instantly. *That is what true creation is all about.*

When you bear witness to your responses to Life's current events and immediately *retract* what you decided *in the past* about similar events, you give yourself almost unimaginable power—including the power to end struggle and suffering forever.

Buddha demonstrated this precisely, and taught it.

~~

It is Gratitude that gives you this power. Gratitude gives you a Fresh Start. It is like being born again, and having the Mind reset to zero. (We'll discuss that in just a bit.) It wipes the slate clean of all prior negative judgments that you may have held about any person, event, circumstance, or situation.

At the risk of a little Repetition right here, let's review from a slightly different angle how the whole Process of Life works, so that you can see all of this even more clearly:

Within an astonishingly short period of time following your birth, you came into contact with—then analyzed, assembled, and stored—a monumental amount of data about your exterior world. You did this so efficiently that after only a few years on this planet, it became almost impossible for you to encounter any new experiences. New *events,* yes. New *experiences,* no.

This is by design.

You are not *supposed* to encounter new experiences. You are supposed to encounter *the same experiences over and over again.*

The experiences you are encountering repeatedly are inside of you, not outside of you. *All* experience is interior. It is *events* that are exterior. But events have nothing to do with your experience. The proof of this is the fact that two people can have distinctly *different* experiences of *the exact same event.*

So we see that you can encounter any number of new exterior *events,* but one can have virtually no truly new *experiences.* And the older you become, the more this will be obvious to you. Indeed, this truth will evidence itself exponentially as each year goes by.

You have *already* experienced this.

You have already experienced love, and you will no doubt experience it again. You have already experienced animosity, and you will no doubt experience it again. You have already experienced commitment, and you will no doubt experience it again. You have already experienced betrayal, and you will no doubt experience it again.

You have already experienced disappointment and excitement, agony and ecstasy, frustration and exhilaration, exasperation and exaltation, anger and joy, agitation and peace, loss and gain, fear and fearlessness, cowardice and courage, ignorance and wisdom, blahs and bliss, confusion and clarity, and just about every other emotional polarity that one could describe or imagine.

> *A Soul Knowing:*
> All experience is interior. It is events that are exterior.

The reason it was said that all experience is interior is that *emotion is the sponsor* of your experience, and all emotions are created within. Events are simply outer physical occurrences. It is the emotion you hold *about* a particular event that creates your experience of it. And there are no new emotions for you to experience at this stage of your life. There is an endless number of unique events which can and will be physically presented to you by Life, but the emotion generated by the event, and the interior experience that this emotion produces, *will be one which you have encountered before*. In most cases, many times before.

～

The Mind remembers its experiences. Every one of them.

Every.

Single.

One.

Of.

Them.

And now we see the reason for this.

Your Mind has been *designed* to hold in memory literally millions of experiences in order for you to notice that you are encountering conditions and events in your exterior world that are the same or nearly the same *in their emotional content* as you have encountered before.

The noticing of this is, in turn, intended to offer you repeated chances—literally *millions* of chances—to respond differently to conditions and events (both past and present) should you choose to, thereby *recreating yourself anew* in the next grandest version of the greatest vision ever you held about Who You Are.

We see, then, that a single Life offers in miniature what reincarnation offers in "maximature": limitless opportunities to evolve.

This is the Process of Life in all its forms.

Scientists tell us that even the Universe is evolving. Do you imagine that you are not?

28

Enlarging the Challenge—*Voluntarily*

WHAT HAS JUST BEEN SAID is that, just when you have given what has been asked of you—just when you have reached Completion by expressing Divinity fully in one moment—*the Finish Line is moved.*

This is good news? This makes you want to leap out of bed in the morning, a smile on your face, a song in your heart, saying that you just can't wait to get into the day?

Well, actually, yes.

When you are clear about why you are here, where you are going, and how this process called "evolution" *works* . . . then, actually, yes, it *is* good news. Because you remember how incredibly . . . *incredible* . . . you felt when you reached that point of Completion in the previous stages of your growth.

You remember the warmth, the bliss, the wonderment and excitement, the quiet elation and gentle, inner satisfaction that washed over you in that moment when you expressed, fully, the love, the understanding, the wisdom and clarity, the compassion and caring, and each of the other Aspects of Divinity (one at a time, or all at once) being placed by you into the life of another and of all others whose lives you touch at the highest level.

You remember that feeling, and *that is a feeling you want again.* That is *an experience you wish to repeat.*

That is the Sense of Your Self that you *have always known is You*. It is Who You Are and How You Are when you are at your very, very best—and you want *more* of that.

Life's answer to your wanting more of that is the glory, the wonder, and the joy of Reliable Repetition.

⌇

Repeating an experience over and over again *in the same way* is not what is meant by the word "more" in this context. You don't merely want "more of the same," you want a *greater degree* of what you experienced before.

Think of it this way: When you were small, the toddlers' rides at the amusement part were fun for sure, and the kids' roller coaster brought you thrills galore—until it didn't anymore. Sooner or later you wanted to try the Big Dipper.

And imagine this: you got on it *voluntarily*.

You watched the others screaming while they were on it. You felt the nervousness in your own stomach as you approached the ticket booth. Yet you bought your ticket anyway, and *you got on it voluntarily*.

⌇

Now that's an analogy, but it's not so very far from what's going on in your life. For *it is the nature of Life to seek greater and greater expressions and experiences of Itself*.

Still, it really *is* time for the struggle to be over. A thrilling challenge is one thing; struggle is another.

Enough is enough. And so a way has been found for the journey to continue, but for the struggle to be over. Tools have been given to you. One of them is The Law of Retraction, powered by Gratitude.

Using this tool takes you to the next stage on your Sacred Journey. It is the next step to mastery. Mastery is when the challenges become greater, but the struggle disappears.

If you have been suffering, it is not because you have been following The Path of the Soul. It is because you have taken a detour along a trail that led you away from The Path, forgetting to remember who you really are, why you are here, and where you were intending to go.

The Path of the Soul does not require or include suffering. The way for the struggle to be over is to *stay on The Path.* Gratitude returns you there. It speeds you in your evolution. It's the fast track.

⌒

You do not have to expand or grow or evolve at any particular rate, however. You can go through one entire lifetime reacting the same way to the same kinds of events. Many people do. *Most* people do. Only those who are deeply committed to growth, to their own personal and spiritual evolution, would spend the time and energy on choosing and changing their emotions—shifting from anger or frustration to Gratitude, for instance—in order to produce new and grander experiences of themselves.

> *A Soul Knowing:*
> Mastery is when the challenges become greater, but the struggle disappears.

This requires a very high-level promise to oneself. It entails an acknowledgment that there is something Larger going on here—something more than just day-to-day Life, rolling out randomly. It implies that there is a Particular Process taking place in a Particular Way. A sacred process. An eternal process. A process that serves a Divine Purpose—all of which is described in wonderful detail in Chapter 14.

Your commitment to this Process and this Purpose is your own shouting out, it is your own full-voiced declaration to the world: "My life really *is* about more than just get the guy, get the girl, get the car, get the job, get the house, and get all the stuff everyone else is trying to get! I will *not* spend my time on the 98% of things that *just don't matter.* I . . . will . . . not."

29

Can Emotions Be Selected?

IF GRATITUDE IS a powerful tool that can change your experience of life by allowing you to focus on The Only Thing That Matters, the question then becomes: What could cause you to decide to feel Gratitude in the face of events or conditions that ordinarily would invite condemnation, not commendation? How do you put the power to use?

As we explore this answer, you're invited to notice the specific words that were used in the question: "What could cause you *to decide to feel* Gratitude . . . ?"

Decide? Emotions are things we decide to feel?

Yes.

～

Emotions are not what your experiences generate; they are what generate your experiences.

Most people don't understand this. Nor do most people see themselves as having an active role in choosing their emotions. Not at first, in any event. They may feel that they can *control* their emotions by choosing something *other* then the emotion that arose initially, but most people do not feel that they are creating their first response. At first, they say, their emotions simply arise. They *show up*. Unannounced. Unbidden. Unexpectedly, sometimes.

People think of themselves as just *having* an emotional response. They often say that they were just *overcome* by emotion.

The truth is that all emotions are chosen—even first ones. The Mind *decides* to feel a certain way. Emotions are an Act of Will.

This is a challenging truth to embrace. Accept this and suddenly you're responsible for everything: for how you feel, for how you act with others as a result of how you feel, and for how all events in your life are experienced. So when people hear this, they often look for an "out."

("There must be *some* way in which I am not responsible for how I'm feeling. I mean, I can see that I'm responsible for what I *do* with my feelings, but my feelings themselves? *C'mon!* I can't be responsible for *that*. I feel the way I *feel*, and that's *just my truth*. Am I supposed to *lie* about that? Am I to be *inauthentic?"*)

Have you ever told yourself (or sold yourself) some version of that? Most people have. Yet the human race can never evolve until we see the role we all play in the creation of our emotions. The story we've been telling ourselves about emotions is our admission that we have no idea how the Mind really works. The extraordinary description of the Mechanics of the Mind found in *When Everything Changes, Change Everything* is reprinted here, virtually verbatim, as it offers deep insight that cannot be repeated too often.

This book tells us that emotions are chosen. They are selected exactly the way you select the clothes you want to wear. Emotions are the costumes of the Mind. The Mind *decides* to feel a certain way.

Now this much will be conceded: Your Mind makes its decision *so fast* that it can *seem* as though you have no control over your emotions at all. At least not your very first reactions.

Your Mind moves you very quickly into an emotion, based on a Thought that it has formed. This is what is meant when people say, "I felt very moved." Indeed, they were.

Thought is *energy*, and your Mind's job is to *move that energy into motion* (E+motion).

Since this happens so *lightning* fast, it becomes crucial that we know, *ahead of time,* before we are confronted with an "emotional situation," *what makes us choose one emotion over another.*

You've already learned that it is your Thought. Yet what *generates* the Thought that creates an Emotion? Where does any particular Thought *come from?*

If you can figure *that* out, you will have gone a long way toward being able to *change* your Thought about something. And if you can change your Thought about something, you can create a different Emotion around it—which will produce a different Experience of it.

~

So here's how it all works: The moment your Mind encounters anything in your exterior world, using the sensing instrument that is your Body, your Mind will collect the Data it is receiving and search its memory for any correlating Data. It will then compare what is happening Now with what its memory holds about any similar prior event, and use this combined Data to form your present Truth about the event now occurring in your exterior world.

> *A Soul Knowing:*
> All emotions are chosen. They are an act of Will.

Your Truth about it will be drawn mostly from your *past,* and least of all from what is *actually happening right now.* This is because what is happening now is but one byte of Data, compared to the megabytes of Data your Mind holds about similar prior events. "Now" is simply overwhelmed by "Then." Today becomes deeply mired in Yesterday.

The Truth that your Mind forms in this way creates your Thought about what is now occurring. This can be either an Imagined Truth, the Apparent Truth, or the Actual Truth, depending on the quality of the Data The Mind has accessed.

Your Thought will quickly generate an Emotion, and that Emotion will very rapidly produce your Experience. All of this, in fact, happens in one-millionth of a second. You will then call the Experience you arrived at in this way, "Reality."

It is *by this process* that "you create your own reality."

Now just think: if you were to change the Data of your Mind *ahead of time* about *all of your past* (using the Law of Retraction), you could rise to a new level of preparedness to experience mastery *in this Moment*—because whether your Mind is caught up in memories of the past, or you are deeply engaged in a challenging Present Moment and wish to change your Mind *this instant* about it using the same tool, you will in each case encounter Gratitude. And *that is transformative.*

~

What has been labeled the New Thought Movement has been saying for years, "You create your own reality," but sadly, it has not explained very clearly how you are doing it.

Reality Creation goes far beyond simple "positive thinking" or the making of "affirmations"—approaches that have been touted as the "secret" to producing what one desires.

That's child's play. It is the sandbox of metaphysics. And so, of course, in movies and books about Life's big "secret," these simplistic approaches are shown manifesting simple toys.

If you really want to know how to create your Highest Experience of Self (and not just put a new car in the driveway), if you really want to create a better world (and not just a better necklace for your bodice), you will benefit enormously from an understanding of the Mechanics of the Mind as outlined in short form above.

(As mentioned before, a rich, wonderfully clear and far more detailed explanation of this can be found in the book *When Everything Changes, Change Everything,* from Hay House, 2010.)

~

As fast as the Mind works, it still works only on the Data it is working *with*. Computer programmers are very familiar with this concept: GIGO.

Garbage in/garbage out.

So if you have put "garbage" *into* your Mind (about Life, about God, about any particular experience that you have stored in your virtually endless memory), garbage is what is going to come *out* of your Mind about anything in the Present Moment that even *looks like* a previous experience (and all of them do, in one way or another). Yet if you have put Gratitude in, then Gratitude is what is going to come out.

It's still GIGO!

What we are saying here is that if you *live in Gratitude* for *all* events, then Gratitude for every one of your Present Moment events will arise—*regardless of the event itself.*

~

The employing of Gratitude as a tool is what separates the Master (who always does so) from the Serious Student (who occasionally does so), and the Serious Student from the Initiate (who has not yet even heard of it in this context—or who has heard of it, but who uses it very rarely, if at all.)

The Master understands that every event in Life is part of a Contextual Field (explained here in Chapter 14) creating a space within which to express the next grandest version of the greatest vision that the Master ever held about who the Master is and chooses to be.

The Master, therefore, says yes and only yes to every experience. And the Master says it joyfully, gratefully, for the Master knows that a glorious moment has arrived that is perfect for the glorious expression and experience of Glory Itself, called Divinity.

How can the Master be anything but grateful for this? And when the Master knows that everything occurring has been co-created by many Souls, working in collaboration and agreement with the Master's own Soul, to produce the circumstance or condition currently presenting itself, how can the Master complain? Of what would the Master disapprove?

30

Knowing About the Tool and Using It Are Two Different Things

PLEASE DON'T BE SATISFIED with simply knowing about this marvelous transformational tool called Gratitude. Make a commitment to *use this tool yourself.* You will see how the energy you may be carrying about any unwelcome event, past or present, can be transformed in the blink of an eye.

Simply say *Thank you, God,* the moment any so-called "negative" event occurs today or presents itself in your memory. Then decide immediately what you are thanking God *for.*

Say, "Thank you, God, for giving me this chance—yes, even one *more* chance—to heal my thought that . . ." or " . . . to change my old story about . . ." or " . . . to release my fears around . . . "—or *however* you want to use this Reliable Repetition of a Revolving Emotion.

Decide then and there Who You Are and Who You Choose To Be in relationship to the event or circumstance currently arising.

Here now are some additional examples of how you may wish to use the tool of Gratitude to allow you to focus your daily life more clearly and consistently on The Only Thing That Matters.

The Morning Prayer

Make it your habit to say to yourself each day as you awaken:

Thank you, God, for another day and another chance to be my Highest Self.

Do this *first thing,* before thinking or doing anything else. After about a week or so it will become second nature. Saying this as you are rising is a wonderful way to plant the seed in your Mind, as a First Thought, that Life is something to be grateful for *precisely because of the opportunity it gives you* to move into the next greatest expression of your Highest Idea about You.

It tells your Mind that you know what the day's events are about, even before they occur, and that this knowing allows you to be grateful *in advance* for what will follow.

Such an announcement does more than merely put you in a good frame of mind. If you believe that what you Thought about Life has at least some effect on how Life plays itself out, you must surely see that beginning each day with such a remarkable statement of faith in the Process of Life Itself becomes *formative* in the Process of Life Itself.

It has been said that Life informs Life about Life through the Process of Life Itself. If this is true (and it is), you are doing more with this little morning prayer than saying what you expect. You are declaring what you choose to co-create. Such a declaration is neither pointless nor meaningless.

~

The Solution Prayer

Should your day present you with an experience or circumstance that you consider problematic, and if you find yourself paying more than a little mental attention to it, try saying this:

Thank you, God, for helping me to understand that this problem has already been solved for me.

This is one of the most powerful prayers you could ever use, because it *presumes the outcome.* It is not a request or a supplication, but a pure and simple statement of assured awareness of What Is So.

Praying a prayer of supplication declares your lack of assurance regarding results. It is not necessary to ask for something you already have. Therefore, if you ask for something, you are as much as announcing that you may or may not get it.

Saying thanks for something before you get it is a declaration of absolute clarity that you are going to receive it. This shift of energy is neither pointless nor meaningless.

The Perfection Prayer

Whatever shows up in your Life, allow yourself to "see the Perfection." Express your sincere gratitude with this:

Thank you, God, for the Perfection of this outcome, of this moment, and of my Life.

Try to remain in that state of Gratitude until it becomes "really Real," not "pretend Real." This is about calling forth a feeling.

Sometimes people say things in prayer that they wish were real, but that they do not truly believe. That's okay. That's perfectly normal. But a statement of what you choose to be real can *become* real through the simple act of your choosing it, and continuing to choose it.

Now here's a little trick. After you choose it, allow yourself to feel it. Close your eyes and open your Mind and allow the feeling of perfection regarding the moment and your whole life to permeate your entire Body. Breathe slowly and deeply—nice, long, easy breaths—three times as you do this. By the end of the third breath, you should be starting to feel the

Peace of Perfection. If it helps, picture soft golden light surrounding you while you do the breathing.

Since all experience is internal and all events and circumstances are only external, continuing to use Gratitude to see Perfection adds to the data in your Mind, which impacts your Truth about an event or circumstance, which creates a Thought about it, which generates an Emotion regarding it, which produces an Experience of it—and, once again, this Experience will be your interior Reality.

You have taken an exterior occurrence and you have literally internalized it. Such a process can turn your world *inside out.*

～

It would be silly to suggest that it is always easy to "see the Perfection." It is extremely challenging when what is happening seems anything *but* Perfect. The death of a loved one, the loss of a job, and the end of a relationship would surely all qualify as events in that category. And there are many others that could be brought to Mind. So you may need assistance with this. And where can it be found?

Try this. It is the theory here that one's idea of Perfection is going to depend a great deal on one's idea of the Self, and on one's reason for being on the earth. It is these ideas that produce one's understanding of Divine Perfection, one's clarity about *What One Desires,* and from this, the mental peace that creates the end to struggle and suffering—an outcome for which all of humanity yearns.

These thoughts must come first. You must be clear about your idea of Self and your reason for being on the earth, or placing labels of Perfection on calamitous events will only anger the Mind and shut it down, turning you away from The Only Thing That Matters.

31

The Biggest Choice You Will Ever Make

Your idea of the Self and of your reason for being on the earth breaks down, ultimately, to two simple choices. These were succinctly described in the book referenced earlier, *The Storm Before the Calm,* which laid it out this way:

Choice #1

You could conceive of yourself as a Chemical Creature, or a "Logical Biological Incident." That is, the logical outcome of a biological process engaged in by two other biological processes, called mother and father.

If you see yourself as a Chemical Creature you would see yourself as having no more connection to the Larger Processes of Life than any other chemical or biological life form.

Like all the others, you would be impacted *by* life, but could have very little impact *on* life. You certainly couldn't create events, except in the most remote, indirect sense. You could create more *life* (all chemical creatures carry the biological capacity to re-create more of themselves), but you could not create what life *does,* or how it "shows up," in any given moment.

Further, as a Chemical Creature you would understand yourself to have very limited ability to create an intentioned *response* to the events and conditions of life. You would see yourself as a creature of habit and instinct, with only those resources that your fundamental biology provides you.

You would see yourself as having more resources than a turtle, because your biology has gifted you with more. You would see yourself as having more resources than a butterfly, because your biology has gifted you with more.

You would see yourself as having more resources than an ape or a dolphin (but, in those cases, perhaps not all that *many* more), because your biology has gifted you with more. Yet that is all you would see yourself as having in terms of resources.

You would see yourself as having to deal with life day by day, pretty much as it comes, with perhaps a tiny bit of what seems like "control" based on advance planning, etc., but you would know that at any minute anything could go wrong—and often would.

Choice #2

You could conceive of yourself as a Spiritual Being inhabiting a biological mass—what is called a physical body.

If you saw yourself as a Spiritual Being, you would see yourself as having powers and abilities far beyond those of a simple Chemical Creature— powers that transcend basic physicality and its laws.

You would understand that these powers and abilities give you some collaborative control over the *exterior* elements of your Individual and Collective Lives, and complete individual control over the *interior* elements—which means that you have total ability to create your own reality, because your reality has nothing to do with *producing* the exterior elements of your lives and everything to do with how you *respond to* the elements that have been produced.

Also, as a Spiritual Being, you would know that you are here (on the earth, that is) for a spiritual reason. This is a highly focused purpose and has nothing to do directly with your occupation or career, your income or possessions or achievements or place in society, or *any* of the exterior conditions or circumstances of your life.

You would know that your purpose has to do with your *interior* life—and that how well you do in *achieving* your purpose may very often have an *effect* on your exterior life.

~

The presumption at this stage is that you have already selected Choice #2. It is highly unlikely that you would have read this far if you had not. Yet merely making this choice is not enough.

Some human beings make this choice consciously, seeing and embracing themselves as Spiritual Beings, but then don't really believe that they are—or are not sure.

Some human beings make this decision consciously and are sure about it, but then don't know how to implement it in their lives.

Some human beings make this decision consciously, are sure about it, and know how to implement it in their lives, but don't do so.

Some human beings make this decision consciously, are sure about it, know how to implement it in their lives, and do so—but then *don't,* and then do again, and then don't again . . . so they experience their spiritual identity as an on-again-off-again thing.

It is for all of these reasons that the world is the way it is today.

~

The challenge, if you are to find peace and end the struggle and suffering in your life, is to embrace your identity as a Spiritual Being, and then implement that choice consistently.

As has been stated here now many times, most people don't know what that "looks like."

We are about to show you more of that, and how you can bring that more fully into your own life, using some marvelous tools. You've already remembered Gratitude. Now let's look at some other tools as well.

32

Another Gift, Another Tool

A SECOND VALUABLE ITEM for your tool chest is called . . .

RECONTEXTUALIZATION

Using this remarkable device, you dramatically alter the Data that gives rise to a Truth that forms the Thought that produces the Emotion that creates your Experience of any Present Moment.

The process of Recontextualization does just what its name suggests. It creates a new context within which to frame Life Itself, as well as any event or circumstance within Life, virtually eliminating any reason or justification you might have felt in your life to be angry or resentful with or about anyone.

This remarkable tool involves a repositioning of your perspective, allowing you to see what is going on at any moment in your Life within a new and startlingly different context.

Let's back up here and begin at the beginning on this one.

~

It should be clear at this point in your life that what brings you joy—the *highest* joy—is self-expression. It is through the fullest expression of Self that the fullest experience of Who You Really Are is achieved. Now, a person looking at Life a certain way might feel that the fullest expression of Self is very wonderful if it can be made to happen, but that it doesn't happen very often for many, and that Life has more to it than this, and that we must all go on, whether we feel "fully self-expressed" or not.

Recontextualization, on the other hand, tells you that *full self-expression* is the experience *you came for.* This creates a not-willing-to-settle-for-anything-less thought in your Mind. It reformulates the days and times of your Life within the context of your Soul's Agenda, not your Mind's concepts. The Soul's Agenda always exceeds the Mind's Concepts. This is not true some of the time, this is true all of the time.

~

What is being said here is that Recontextualization dares you, calls you, invites you, empowers you to see your Life in a new way—to give it a different meaning, to surround it with a different purpose, to place it in an entirely different context.

It invites you to place yourself in the center of the Wheel of Creation, and to envision your Self as collaborating with other Souls all around you in the producing of conditions and circumstances that are ideal for the Completion of your purpose in placing yourself in any Present Moment.

> *A Soul Knowing:*
> *Full self-expression* is
> the experience *you*
> *came for.*

It invites you to place that purpose itself into a new context: the Agenda of your Soul and the Sacred Journey upon which your Soul has embarked. This is truly seeing your life and its every event in a new way.

With Recontextualization can come a sudden reactualization of the Self. And as you become a self-actualized being, rather than a reactive being, everything changes in the way you move through the world.

Let's look at just one example. After using the tool of Recontextualization, you never again "work" at a job you don't like, and you never again "don't like" a job at which you are working. That is because your "work" has become a "joy"—even *if it's the same job you had before.*

What has happened is that you have reframed your whole idea of what "work" is about. You have *recontextualized it.* Before, you thought work was about "earning your keep," paying the bills, being "responsible," and "doing what you have to do" to stay alive and take care of those you love. Now you know it's about making a *life* rather than a living. It is about you as a spiritual being, not what your business card says, and it is suddenly this that matters.

Your work is simply a means to an end; it's a way of your being what your spiritual journey is inviting you to be. It is merely providing you with a context within which to be that, nothing more.

What aspect of Divinity are you demonstrating—to yourself and through yourself—when you're taking care of those you love? What aspect are you expressing when you pay bills that you owe and acquire things that you need or desire?

What aspect of Godliness are you exhibiting when you give to charity, or offer financial assistance to someone you know who is in need? What about when you purchase a wonderful gift for a loved one?

Look at what you do with your money. This is who you are.

You are not your job. Your job simply provides you the means with which to be who you are. Are you generous, giving, caring? Are you fair, honest, trustworthy? Are you protective, empowering, creative?

All these things are aspects of Divinity that you give yourself the ability to express freely, through the gift that Life has given you of what you call "work."

When you see your job in this way, you will experience it not as something that you *have* to do (there are many people who choose not to work), but as part of a larger process by means of which you get to *be* particular aspects of Divinity that you have freely decided to be.

For some, this is a new way of looking at employment for sure—but *that is what Recontextualization is all about.*

Interestingly, you don't even have to have an affinity for what you're doing in *any* given moment, not just at work, for this tool to be effective. It could, indeed, be that job you don't particularly like, but it could also be a home chore with which you are bored, a task you would rather not do, a conversation you wish you did not have to have, an evening you had hoped to avoid—it could be anything. Again, it is suddenly not what you are *doing* that matters; it is the decision you have made about *What One Desires,* and your close look at how you can manifest that through *whatever* you are doing. This becomes The *Only* Thing That Matters.

This is how you can Recontextualize any Moment. You simply decide that it exists for a reason entirely different from the reason that you had given it before.

Magically, that new choice—if it is your highest choice—can impact and affect what you are doing in such a way that the actual *doing of it* becomes a pleasure and a joy.

You can find it joyful to wash dishes when coming from this place. You can find it easy, and actually wonderful, to go to a job that you once hated to go to when coming from this place.

Returning to the motherhood example, this is the place that a mother comes from when she changes and nurses her two-month-old baby at 3:30 in the morning. Bringing herself out of a sound sleep is probably not what she most wants to do in the middle of the night, but she consciously or unconsciously recontextualizes her activity in a way that permeates her thoughts about herself and about what is going on—and this process is so powerful that she finds she actually *does* want to do what she is doing.

Conversations with God tells us that "no one does anything they don't want to do." Recontextualization takes you to the heart of that truth. People can *think* that they don't want to do it by forgetting the reason why it *benefits* them to do it, then imagining themselves to be the *victims* of having to do it, through a circumstance that they, themselves, helped to co-create *in order* to experience the benefit that they now cannot see.

Recontextualization places you back into the original space, the space of your Soul's first purpose. It replaces Original Sin with Original Motivation. This truly is an amazing grace, for once you were blind, but now you see.

~

Using Recontextualization, you realize that what*ever* is happening right now is happening in order to provide a context within which you can be and experience the next grandest version of the greatest vision you ever held about Who You Are. This exceptional tool is another way of focusing on The Only Thing That Matters.

Of course you now know—thanks to the "remembering" you have done here—*that this is not mandatory.* This has been said over and over again, so that you can be very, very clear about that. If you choose to side-step the expression of Divinity at its next highest level, finding it more of a challenge than you wish to encounter in this or any particular Moment, you may experience the Moment in any way that you wish.

> *A Soul Knowing:*
> No one does
> anything they don't
> want to do.

So now the question is put to you that all spiritual masters face. (Not that you suddenly have to become a spiritual master, but it may serve you to look at, once in a while, a question that they look at all the time.) The question: If it is *you* choosing, in your own Mind, to have one particular interior experience rather than a different interior experience regarding an Outer Event in your life, how can you not be content and okay no matter what is being experienced? Are you not getting your way? Even if you are experiencing being scared, or angry, or frustrated, or upset . . . are you not getting your way? Or is it still your continuing belief that you do not choose your emotions, and that you have no control over them?

You do have control, of course. You select, create, and then act on every emotion you ever have. What you select, when you create it, and how you act on it is solely up to you. No one can make you have any particular emotion. And knowing this, embracing it, results from a growth in Consciousness arising out of your use of the Soul's tools of Gratitude and Recontextualization. These tools produce a shift of attitude, not of circumstance. *Nothing has changed, but everything is different.*

What has been altered is not the exterior, but the interior. Now you are internally clear that you are *always at choice* regarding your Experience of any and every Event or Circumstance, knowing that your Experience is based on Emotions about that Event or Circumstance, arising out of your Thoughts about that Event or Circumstance, emerging from your Truth about that Event or Circumstance, produced by the Data that you hold about that Event or Circumstance—*which Data can, upon your decision, be expanded at any time to include the Awareness of the Soul.*

With such an expansion of the Mind's Data, you become instantly clear that nothing can be forced upon you, *ever,* and that how you are experiencing Life is how you choose to.

You can peer down the throat of the lion without fear, or recoil at the sight of a spider. You can walk the ledge without trembling, or you can shrink from walking out of your own house.

The choice is yours. It has always been yours. The world can do things *to* you, but it cannot extract things *from* you that you do not choose to give.

A steady focus on The Only Thing That Matters, using powerful tools such as Gratitude and Recontextualization, places you in the space of royalty, as the sovereign of your own Kingdom.

Your Kingdom has come, your Will is being done, on earth, which is part of heaven.

Has it not been written: "Ye are Gods"?

33

How High Is the Bar?

Now a word here, please, about expectations. Specifically, those you set for yourself.

Part Two of this text established very clearly where your Soul intends the Sacred Journey to take you. But be careful that you do not "set the bar" too high in terms of how or when you get there.

Your goal is Completion, but that does not mean that you have to show up as a mistake-avoiding, humanity-denying, wisdom-speaking guru every moment of your Life. In fact, everything you do moves you forward on the path of evolution, so do not berate or beleaguer yourself for "not doing it right" as you move through your days and times.

Make ample use of this third Tool for Life . . .

COMPASSION

Remember that Completion was defined as The Totality of You expressing and experiencing Divinity at the highest level that the circumstance, condition, or event of a Present Moment allows, given your level of Consciousness in that Moment.

The final phrase in that last sentence is not unimportant. It would be highly beneficial for you to wrap your understanding of the Sacred

Journey in those words. Nothing will cause you to feel waylaid faster than expecting the impossible of yourself.

Remember what Divinity Itself expects of you.

Nothing.

Nothing at all.

You are not required to be or do anything, and nothing is demanded of you. The entire Process of Life is an exercise in Free Will.

And Free Will means exactly that. It does not mean that you are free to do or not do what someone has told you that "God commands." It means you are free to express and experience all of Life exactly as you chose, and there will be no "judgment" or "punishment" involved.

~

It will take some time, in earthly terms, for the New Mind to include in its database the Soul's Awareness. Your Old Mind has, after all, been inundated with all manner of Temporal Truth, which is quite different from Spiritual Reality.

> *A Soul Knowing:*
> Everything you do moves you forward on the path of Evolution.

At first, you may want to deny your Soul's Awareness. Ironically—considering that you have told yourself that all of Life's Truths emerge from an all-loving God—you may tell yourself that the Eternal Awareness brought to you by your Soul is, actually, too good to be true. It seems incredible, on the surface, that you have truly been given absolute freedom to make your decisions and to create your life as you choose.

As well, a human being's level of Consciousness (or, to use our "sponge" analogy, the ability of your Mind to absorb your Soul's Awareness) will most likely be different at age 7 from what it will be at 47 or 67. (Not necessarily, but most likely.)

To make the illustration more immediate, your own level of Consciousness could be remarkably different tomorrow from what it is today. And, for that matter, in the next *instant* from what it is right now—*perhaps even as a result of reading this.* (Wisdom which you have brought *to* yourself *from* yourself *through* yourself.)

Know, too, that Consciousness *fluctuates.* It does not remain constant simply because it has reached a certain level, but increases and decreases depending upon the amount of the Soul's Awareness that is integrated into the Mind's Experience at any given Moment.

Or as one observer put it: "Enlightenment is not like getting your tonsils out—once it's done, it's done. Enlightenment is a moment-to-moment experience. That is both its challenge and its delight. The Quest is never over, and it is never boring."

Yet there is a way to put an end to the "wild swings" from extremely high Consciousness to very low Consciousness that you may have encountered on your Sacred Journey. That way is to use the tool of Compassion when you observe yourself expressing less than your highest Consciousness.

Allow yourself to notice that you are just as you need to be, just when you need to be, in order to move forward the agenda of your Soul.

You are learning how to do that—or, more correctly, *remembering* what your Soul already knows about that. *Conversations with God* says something quite remarkable on this. It says that it is impossible for you to make a mistake. It is only possible to take steps that continue to lead you to your destination.

A true scientist never becomes discouraged for long (if she becomes discouraged at all) working in a laboratory and failing to get the desired results. The scientist understands perfectly that the more sophisticated the experiment, the more *nuanced* each step in the experiment must be. The slightest shade of a difference in approach, or in any of the many variable aspects, and the outcome can be vastly altered. Yet each approach leads toward the scientist's desired destination.

Your life is exactly like that. Your actions—even those you would label as errors—could not be more perfect to ignite your remembrance of all that you choose to remember, to experience all that you choose to experience, to get you to all the places you choose to go, through the blessed expression of Life Itself.

So then, each time your experience shows you the next step on your path, allow your heart to open, not close, knowing that Heaven is at work here, and all will be well.

Poet Em Claire has written of this, too . . .

Please do not regret
all those moments that have brought you
Here.
If you are reading this,
then your perseverance has been answered,
and a Grace is coming.
So for now, hold on loosely to where you are.
And like knots on a rope that mark your reaching,
hand over hand
you will continue to climb—
sometimes through ecstasy,
sometimes through white agony, but
higher
into evermore light.
This same formula over
and over again.
Until that day you find yourself
just a beacon;
only flame.
In a place
where even Love Itself has come undone.

———

"Love Itself"
© 2006 em claire

Dear Sweet, Wonderful One . . .

Know that the Soul's intention is never to bring you to the breaking point, but always to invite you to the breakthrough point. On your way there, be gentle with yourself. Be soft and understanding and kind, and use this tool of Compassion.

Remember what was said in the very early going of this exploration: *You are doing nothing wrong.*

You are simply remembering. And you cannot remember all of the Soul's wisdom at once. You really do have to ring out the sponge every now and then if you wish to absorb the ocean.

Your present level of Consciousness is therefore not a measure of your goodness as a human being, nor of your credentials as a spiritual entity.

A third grader is no less a beautiful child than a fourth grader, and no less a picture of perfection than a college graduate. And one who has slipped and fallen and gotten up again has had to call forth more courage than one who, while still brave enough to be taking a challenging journey, has never scraped a knee.

So have Compassion for yourself. You are courageous and good, and you deserve it.

~

And while you are using this wonderful tool, please be sure to direct it to others as well. They, too, are just now remembering. And some of them have not yet remembered as much as you.

One of the highest uses of Compassion you could ever devise will be your employment of it with everyone whose life touches yours.

Many will come to you with their anger, their upset, their injury, their neediness. Many will call on you in their moments of dysfunction and their "cloud of unknowing." In their confusion, some of them will actually imagine that they need you, you, and *only you* to heal their wounds and to bring them what they have not yet learned how to give to themselves: Love and understanding.

And acceptance. And patience. And forgiveness.

The more often you use Compassion to offer others these gifts, the greater will be your familiarity with this remarkably healing tool—and you will then find it easier to use on *yourself.*

~

Compassion is not always easy to give to oneself. Many people find they are not comfortable receiving this from themselves. It interrupts their "story" of "never doing it right" or "being at fault" or "falling short" or "not being good enough." They feel that by being compassionate with themselves they are letting themselves "off the hook," or giving themselves "a pass" regarding something they should continue to feel bad about.

So to be tough on themselves, they decline to offer themselves Compassion.

This allows many people who have felt bad about themselves for "not doing it right" since childhood to continue to do so. In this, they are their own hardest taskmaster. Or, as the late Walt Kelly famously said through the voice of his beloved comic strip character *Pogo:* "We have met the enemy, and he is us."

> *A Soul Knowing:*
> Compassion
> generates clarity.

Finally, after treating themselves this way for years, the only way many people can *ever* feel comfortable using the tool of Compassion is to use it on others. Often it's hard for them to even find the tool . . . it's been so long since they've used it. Yet the miracle of Compassion is that if you even find the edge of it, if you even touch the tip of it, the iceberg melts. The effect is instant.

The heart opens.

And suddenly, when the heart opens, the Mind opens. It can hear things it could not hear before. Like the soft voice of the Soul, gently offering a larger view, a deeper understanding, a grander perspective—and quietly engaging a different agenda, a new priority, an altered purpose. Immediately, in the space of Compassion, what really *matters* becomes clear.

Nobody who sits in the seat of Compassion finds themselves focused on irrelevant things. *Compassion generates clarity.*

~

So use this gifting tool often. You will find that its effect is circular. As you give more to yourself, you will have more to give to others. As you give more to others, you will have more to give yourself. You can start at either place.

It is, as all of Life . . . simply another form of Love.

34

A Final Tool

THERE IS ONE MORE TOOL you'll want to know about. It is the final tool that will be described for you here, and it was saved for last because its effect can be perhaps the most profound impact produced by any tool, creating a truly extraordinary effect.

This is a tool that you will use on everyone in your life who has ever done anything in any way negative to you—and you will use it *not* by using it, but by throwing it away.

The tool in question is . . .

FORGIVENESS

Let's begin our description of this tool by looking at what it has in common with all of the others. Every one of the tools that you have been offered here is designed to produce one basic experience: freedom. That is because freedom is the essence of Divinity.

There are a lot of words used to describe the fundamental quality of Divinity in human terms—love, peace, joy, etc.—but the word "freedom" comes closest, perhaps, to capturing the primary quality from which all others flow.

A person who is absolutely and totally free . . . and this does not mean merely being free to do anything he wants anytime, anywhere he wants, but it also means being free of any sorrow or sadness, any struggle or suffering, any wounds or injuries, any tragedy or torment—anything whatsoever in the past that could cloud or diminish or impact in any unpleasant way the Moment that is Present . . . a person who is *this* kind of free would love everybody and everything, always be at peace, inevitably experience joy, be forever captivated by Life's wonder, and feel, from one Moment to the next, simply Divine.

So if the experience of Divinity is your goal—(and it is, whether you have known it or not), then that which produces freedom would be the tools you try to find, so that you might construct your reality (which is totally an inner creation and experience that essentially *determines* what outer events and circumstances mean) in such a way that you would never be unhappy for any reason ever again.

Such a state of being would then allow you to move forward with the Agenda of the Soul, advancing rapidly and reaching Completion on your Sacred Journey, thus using virtually every Moment of your Life to serve the Divine Purpose.

This is the way Lao-tzu lived. This is the way Buddha lived. This is the way Jesus lived. This is the way that all spiritual masters have walked the earth. All of these masters, and many more, have said quite directly, each in their own way, that an achievable goal for all human beings was freedom from suffering—which produced everything else that a holy and good life would allow.

The tools you have been given here do just that. Gratitude will give you freedom from struggle and suffering, *in an instant*. Recontextualization will give you freedom from anger and resentment, *in an instant*. Compassion will give you freedom from self-blame and lack of self-worth, and from frustration with others, *in an instant*. And now your final gift, Forgiveness, will give you freedom from all hurt, damage, or injury in any way from any source.

Forgiveness will give you this on the day that you decide you never have to use it again—on the day that you throw it away. It is the discarding of the tool, not the using of it, wherein which its tremendous power is unleashed—like a coiled spring let out of a box. So perhaps the tool should really be called Forgiveness Forgone.

On the day that you understand that you don't have anyone to forgive—and you *never* had anyone to forgive for anything at all, because all human expressions are ultimately an expression of love, if only in a distorted form, as we discussed in Chapter 16—you will be free, no matter what has occurred in your life. Free from struggle, free from suffering, at last.

This is the kind of freedom that Nelson Mandela felt, allowing him to love the jailers who keep him imprisoned for over 20 years, to use one recent, and striking, human example. This is the kind of freedom that Pope John Paul II felt when he went to the jail cell of the man who shot and nearly killed him, giving the gunman his papal blessing.

What is the secret behind this kind of freedom—a level of freedom which allows its holder to completely set aside Forgiveness as a tool for living?

It is the same secret that allows it to be said that God never forgives anyone for anything. God never has, and God never will.

Conversations with God makes this bold statement, and does it so unequivocally that even those who agree with CWG's other spiritually revolutionary revelations find themselves raising their eyebrows—until they look behind the statement to the explanation that is given.

> A Soul Knowing:
> Forgiveness is not
> necessary.

As we've noted before, God does not and will not offer forgiveness to anyone for anything because *forgiveness is not necessary.* It is replaced in the process of Divine Balance with a more searingly powerful energy: Understanding.

It is because this is such a radical idea, different from just about anything and everything you have ever been taught, that we are revisiting this principle here again, announcing Forgiveness Forgone as one of the powerful tools that you may use to reach Completion on your Sacred Journey. And, the reason, once again . . .

First, Divinity understands Who and What It Is, and so It is Aware that It cannot possibly be hurt or damaged, injured or diminished in any way. This means that Divinity would not be disappointed or frustrated or annoyed or angry or vengeful for any reason. It simply *has* no reason. "Vengeance is mine, sayeth the Lord" is the biggest spiritual untruth of all time.

That needs to be repeated: "Vengeance is mine, sayeth the Lord" is the biggest spiritual untruth of all time.

Second, God understands that humans do *not* understand who and what *they* are, and so imagine that they *can* be hurt and damaged, injured and diminished—and that it is from this experience, or fear, of being hurt that all thoughts, words, and actions seemingly requiring Forgiveness flow. Knowing this, God has no need to *forgive* you (even if God could somehow be "hurt"), any more than you have a need to "forgive" a two-year-old child for saying or doing something that doesn't make sense.

～

The idea that *you* need to forgive somebody is clearly based on the fact that you feel offended, damaged, or hurt by another. Such a thought denies the reality of who you really are.

Nelson Mandela and Pope John Paul II never entered into such denial. (Or if they did, they moved out of it permanently.) While they did not agree with what another had done, they understood why the other did it.

Just as we understand the child whose simple immaturity and confusion led to his actions, so, too, do we see, when we come from the place of Deep Understanding, that the exact same thing is true of the adults who act in ways that persons of lesser awareness might call hurtful or damaging.

Understanding thus replaces Forgiveness in the Mind of those who have expanded their Consciousness to include the Awareness of the Soul. The Soul knows that nobody does anything inappropriate, given their model of the world. The Soul knows that everyone is doing the best they can at any given moment.

A wonderful effort of your Mind, then, each time you begin to feel that you are or have been hurt or damaged in any way, would be to open itself to the wisdom of the Soul.

Stop. Breathe. And then listen.

Listen to the reasoning of the Soul—what has been called SouLogic—and you will move closer and closer to Completion, in that moment, of your Sacred Journey.

～

Publisher's Note: If you would like to see a healing process that has been developed around this particular tool, you may wish to watch a video of the SouLogic Process. It can be found at the following link:

www.TheOnlyThingThatMatters.com/video

35

Mental Emptiness

You may be wondering—if the Mind travels with the Soul between lifetimes, why are you now having to "remember" what you have brought to your own attention here?

The Mind of all human beings is reset to zero at the Moment of Birth. All previous data is deleted. And so, while on your first day of Life your Soul held an *awareness* of All, your Mind held *nothing* at all.

This is not by accident.

Life is designed to give The Totality of You a fresh start with every incarnation. In this way you can re-create yourself anew in the next grandest version of the greatest vision your Soul ever held about Who You Are.

The slate is wiped clean as part of God's biggest gift: Freedom.

Life wants you to have the freedom to make Today's Choices as you wish, unburdened by the decisions of your past, unlimited thanks to the promise of your future, unfettered by the conditions of your humanity, and unleashed thanks to the glory of your Divinity.

~

Now you may recall that early in these explorations we introduced the idea that the Body and the Mind never die, any more than the Soul ever dies, but that they travel with The Totality of You from lifetime to lifetime. So right now you might say: "If the Mind is reset to zero at every birth, it might as *well* die at the end of its previous Life, because what good is it in *this* Life if it carries no memories of what it learned?"

That's a wonderful question that only a person who is deeply pondering these explanations one by one could possibly think to ask. Once again, the part of *you* that is doing *just that* has placed this query before you, so that you leave no stone unturned.

So to restate the question: If the Mind is reset to zero, with all its information from previous lives deleted, isn't that the same as one Mind dying and us being born with another one?

The answer is no. For your Mind, as we described in Chapter 6, is indeed like a computer—only *much, much better.*

As you probably know, on a computer you cannot permanently erase any data. You can send data to "trash"—that is, you can "delete" it—but the word "delete" is really a false promise. You have simply sent your data to a separate location on your hard drive.

This is a location that your operating system is programmed not to scan every time you give it a command, so the system runs faster. For this reason it's a good idea to send unneeded data to the Trash Bin . . . but it's also a good idea to know that it resides there forever.

Read that: *Forever.*

Many a white-collar criminal, who thought that he'd "trashed" certain evidence of his misdeeds, has found to his dismay when the good guys swoop in, confiscate his laptop, and dip into the so-called deleted files, that they found right there everything they needed to send him up the river for a very long vacation.

> *A Soul Knowing:*
> Life wants you to
> have the freedom to
> make today's choices
> as you wish.

Now these days you hear more and more about software that "shreds" data, but this, too, does not really make anything disappear. It simply overwrites the data, adding new and mishmashed data on *top* of it, to make the original data impossible to clearly see. *But it is still there.* ~~It simply looks like this.~~ (And, actually, much worse. You can't read it at all.)

Ah, but your Mind is more efficient than a computer! It can send data to "trash" (it does exactly this with each new birth), but it can reach into its deleted files and pull out even overwritten data (memories of experiences that you've had over and over and over again, from lifetime to lifetime) and decipher it.

In short, you cannot permanently "shred" the Data of the Mind!

What does this mean as a practical matter? It means that while, yes, you begin each new physical life with a "clean slate," giving you the freedom to make here-and-now choices unencumbered by your choices in the past, your Mind can still access Prior Data from previous lifetimes when the Mind determines it is beneficial, and not a hindrance, to do so. Anything that stops growth is considered a hindrance. Anything that serves the continuance of Life is not.

Hence, we've all heard stories of the person who suddenly "knew" how to swim because a child desperately thrashing about in the lake needed saving, or who suddenly "understood," with zero present-life training in advanced psychology, the exact right thing to say to talk a man out of jumping off a bridge.

Yet for all ordinary intents and purposes, the Mind is free of these trillions of bytes of deleted data, having no need whatsoever to bring forward old ideas or information that will not serve you in the Present Moment.

Rising above any old thought that your Mind may have harbored about your inadequacies or failures, your refreshed Mind opens at each birth to the Awareness that your Soul has always held: that you are magnificent.

Do you think it is happenstance that little children think they are wonderful and can do anything and can be anything, and will live forever?

The closer you are to birth, the closer you are to the truth of your Being. With your memory cleared of all your Previous Life Experiences in the Body, you can be of a new Mind about things. And so it is that you have been wisely advised: *Be ye as little children.*

Let this be your mantra, now and forevermore.

See the world with the innocence of children, approach the world with the daring of children, love the world with the readiness of children, heal the world with the purity of children, change the world with the wisdom of children.

Be ye as little children.

36

Sustaining the Connection Between the Mind and the Soul

THE FREEDOM OF CHILDREN to be authentic, pure, and joyful is what you will experience when you focus your life on The Only Thing That Matters. A deep commitment to peer deeply into each Moment to see how best and most completely you might express What One Desires will move you quickly into an Expanded Consciousness, from which all Divinity arises.

Such Expanded Consciousness is what eventuates when your Mind and your Soul co-join, for then Experience meets Awareness. The question is how to create such Meet Ups. The first thing you have to do is eliminate any thought you may be holding that Expanded Consciousness is something reserved for a select few.

Expanded Consciousness is, in fact, very easy to experience, and everyone on the planet has done so. Yes, even children. Perhaps especially little children.

Your next experience of Expanded Consciousness may occur . . .

- In any Moment, as in a "flash"

- Intermittently, during a short but intense period

- Regularly, over months or years

- Continuously, as an ongoing reality across the remainder of your lifetime

People in the first category are sometimes said to have had an "epiphany," and may then become Seekers.

People in the second category are sometimes said to have had an "awakening" (which might be described as sort of a *sustained* epiphany), and may then become Students.

People in the third category are sometimes said to have reached a high level of Consciousness, and may then become Messengers or Teachers.

People in the fourth category are sometimes said to have reached Enlightenment, and may then be called Saints or Gurus or Masters—although they, themselves, would gently resist such honorifics.

As has been shared here now several times, all people have achieved Completion in many Moments on their Sacred Journey of the Soul. The experience of *continuing* to live in that State is what they are after. And that is simply a matter of learning to open a pathway or a channel between the Mind and the Soul, so that the Mind can bring in the Soul *at will*, producing the experience of Expanded Consciousness regularly over many months or years—and ultimately, as a sustaining reality across the largest part of one's life.

> *A Soul Knowing:*
> Expanded
> Consciousness is very
> easy to experience.

The next tool—the final tool we will explore here—offers a way to *sustain* the experience of Mind/Soul Oneness, when the Mind's Experience combines with the Soul's Awareness to produce the experience of Expanded Consciousness.

This experience does not have to look mysterious or mystical, by the way. The Soul uniting with the Mind can happen in quite ordinary ways at quite ordinary times. For instance, you could be having this experience *right now*, as you are reading this book.

All of the tools you have been given here so far are highly effective in connecting your Mind and Soul.

Nothing will bring you the *feeling* in which the Soul lives faster than Gratitude. Nothing will open you to the depth of the Soul's wisdom faster than Recontextualization. Nothing will bring you more of the Soul's infinite peace faster than Compassion. And nothing will express the gift of the Soul's true nature faster than Forgiveness Forgone.

But there is one magical device, not yet mentioned, that will allow you to *sustain* the experiences to which the other tools lead you, and this is our final recommended tool:

MEDITATION

If it seems predictable and almost spiritually trite to mention this here, it is only because this tool has for so long been such a *proven* method of accessing the Awareness of the Soul that everyone recommends it all the time. Its predictability speaks well for its efficacy.

Not a lot of time is going to be spent here, then, endorsing or advocating Meditation. By now you've heard about it from enough people. What you may want to know, though, is how to do it effectively (if you are not already).

There is no One Best Way to meditate. There's not a Single Size Fits All answer to how to best do it. Each person experiences the process differently. But there are some approaches to the use of this tool that you might find interesting to hear about.

There's not a lot "out there" on the subject that can be found on a few pages for quick and easy reference, so we've included in the Addendum here a direct lift from a book mentioned in Chapter 29, *When Everything Changes, Change Everything.*

That spiritual guide contains a description of four different approaches to meditation, and we felt the material offered insights that should be included in this document. It's part of the back batter, though, rather than the main text, so that if you've read the previous book, you won't have to move through the material again to complete your reading here.

If you have *not* read the *Changes* book and you have an interest in seeing if there's a way that Meditation might work for you—or perhaps work better for you—you'll want to take a look at this Addendum to the present book for sure.

The reason that Meditation is such an effective tool in moving you along your Sacred Journey is that it creates an environment within which a connection can be made between the Mind and the Soul.

There are other ways to create such an environment as well, including, but certainly not limited to, prayer, visualization, guided imagery, ecstatic dance, vision questing, fasting, chanting, drumming, and simple quiet contemplation.

> *A Soul Knowing:*
> The Mind was
> not designed to
> function alone.

Prayer is probably the most widely taught method of connecting with Divinity (which is, of course, what connecting with your Soul is all about). Every religion on the planet teaches it. It can be a wonderful way of establishing contact with God, but for many the difference between Prayer and Meditation feels like the difference between calling room service to place an order and listening to a recording of gentle music on earphones. One is a "sending" energy, and one is a "receiving" energy.

Visualization definitely helps to move the Mind from its current pre-occupation to something more profoundly connected with one's desires, and if one's personal desires are identical to *What One Desires* (they are at the deepest level, but they may not be at the surface level), this technique can be very useful as well. It does, however, engage the Mind more actively than most forms of Meditation.

Other avenues to the Soul, such as guided imagery and ecstatic dance, can absolutely bring one closer to the inner peace that can lead to higher awareness, but most people report that this occurs with not quite the dependability or regularity of Meditation. Guided imagery is a form of Meditation that is led by another person, either "live" or on a recording, and so, by its very nature, is not quite as quietly intimate. Ecstatic dance takes you out of your Mind completely, and has been known to lead to sudden bursts of awareness, but, like drumming and chanting, it uses focal centers of the Mind that are not nearly as peacefully engaged as the Mind is in Meditation, when the focus is away from these centers and away from all activity.

So Meditation has been found by the most number of people, most of the time, to be the most beneficial, constructive, potent, and efficacious tool for bringing the Soul into the Mind.

〜

Whatever *you* do, find some way to create the space for your Mind and your Soul to merge, sharing in the wonder of all that you are. The Mind was not designed to function alone.

Your Mind is a marvelous part of you, and nothing that has been said during this entire discourse has been meant to suggest that the Mind is somehow "less than," or inferior to, the Soul. It is not.

Your Mind is a brilliant apparatus, and it serves the function of guaranteeing your physical survival in this lifetime extremely well. In fact, unfathomably well. We still don't fully understand all the ways in which the Mind works. Yet we *have* observed, through simply watching ourselves, that the Mind functions even more brilliantly when it is open to sources of information—what might be called "wisdom"—that are not generated by the memory of its own limited experiences, but by the unlimited awarenesses that lie outside the Mind, but not outside the reach, of the Totality of You.

If survival were your only concern—or even your primary concern—your Mind might be enough for you to move forward with, as you travel through Life. Yet as we have observed earlier, survival is not your primary concern. It is not even your Basic Instinct. It is, therefore, not at the top of your agenda. Completion is. Completion of the Sacred Journey. And for this you need not only the Mind, but the Soul as well.

That is why Meditation, the final tool explored here, is so strongly recommended.

That is also why this whole book was written. The book might very well have been titled *The Soul Also*. It's overarching point—that the Mind and the Soul were designed to function together—is that important.

If you go through life using only, or even primarily, your Body and your Mind, it is like riding a tricycle on two of its wheels. It's going to be very hard to keep your balance.

37

The First Gift

AND SO WITH THESE FIVE marvelous tools you are now able at last to take your mind off of the 98% of things that really don't matter in your life. These include . . .

How much money you earn.

What people think of you.

Whether your work is done.

What your sexual orientation is.

How many mistakes you've made.

Whether you have your finances planned.

Where you will be ten years from now.

Which stocks to buy.

Why the dining room should have cream-colored walls.

If it's time to install new carpeting.

What car to get.

How to invite some people to your party and not others without hurting feelings (even though in truth you don't want the others there).

Where to store the boxes.

Are the grapes organic?

What religion to follow.

What political party to join.

Which pants to wear with what top.

Should you cut your hair?

Why to make the bed every day.

How to make the bed.

How to make more friends.

How to get rid of the ants.

How to work the remote.

What's for dinner.

Whose turn it is to take the garbage out.

Are you having an affair?

And the 1,001 other things that are not listed here, but that crowd your Mind every single day of your life, to the point where it's been months—literally, *months*—since you've asked yourself: *How can I best serve the agenda of my Soul?*

~

"How can you—what?"
  "How can I best serve the agenda of my Soul?"

"What in the world is that? And what does that have to do with how we're going to pay the mortgage? Or with Matilda's pregnancy! Good God, get your head out of the clouds."

~~~

And that's how "real life" can get in the way. That's how what's happening now can look like it has nothing to do with your eternal journey. That's how Everything That's Going On Outside can feel like an obstacle to Everything That's Wanting to Go On Inside. And there's no way you'll be able to use any of those tools consistently (if at all) unless you first give yourself a special gift.

> *A Soul Knowing:*
> God wants for you
> what you want for you.

This gift precedes all the tools, and creates the space for you to be able to use them. It's the very first gift you must give yourself on The Sacred Journey. It's your "ticket to ride."

Many people have sought to find a way to experience the fullness of who they are by taking the Path of the Soul, yet in crucial moments of their lives they have been resistant to stepping onto that path. They know what the path is, or at least surely have some idea about it, but they may find, in that critical moment, that they do not wish to release a particular negative emotion that they are experiencing.

Or, they may be ready to release their negativity, but they find it difficult to surrender fully to The Divine Purpose and embark with total commitment on The Sacred Journey.

These reactions are not uncommon. People sometimes can feel "good" feeling "bad." So the first gift you have to give yourself if you want any of the tools you have been shown here to work is very, very important.

You must be in the possession of this gift if you're going to even see the *potential* of changing a moment, much less your life—to say nothing of actually *doing it,* using the wonderful tools that Life has given you.

The gift you must give yourself is . . .

WILLINGNESS

~

This is the essential ingredient in any truly transformational experience. Without it, nothing we have talked about here will be possible. With it, everything we've described here and more can occur.

So how does one move into Willingness? It's a choice. It is, quite literally, an *Act of Will.* To engage it, one must have will*power.* One must really understand what is meant by the phrase "Free Will."

One must *free one's Will.*

Your Will and God's Will are One. This is another way of saying that God wants for you what you want for you. It is also true that what you want for you, at the deepest part of your being, is what God wants for Divinity Itself.

Divinity and Humanity want the same thing—the highest expression of Life that is possible and conceivable in any given Moment—because Divinity and Humanity *are* the same thing. Yet your human Will can be, in a sense, imprisoned.

You can be closed off, shut down, locked in, trapped by one's view of life, by a stubbornness to "give in" to love, by a refusal to use the Tools of Life that you've been given. You can, for sure, build your own jail, step into it, and close the door behind you.

People do it all the time. Resentment, Anger, Fear, Self-Righteousness, and Closemindedness are the roads they take to their own penitentiary.

People sadly and mistakenly think these pathways will get them to where they earnestly yearn to go: a place of safety.

That's all that any of us can really think about when we're coming from Small Self. All that our Little One wants is safety. We want protection, finally, from Life. We've had enough sadness. We've had enough suffering. We've had enough of being attacked, of being made wrong, of being overwhelmed. Enough, already. Enough.

And so we close the drawbridge, circle the wagons, batten down the hatches, retreat to the fortress of our Mind's limited experience. At least it's familiar territory. At least it's common ground. At least it feels safe for the moment. It may not be fun, it may not be very exciting, it may not offer the glory of arms-wide-open expansion or the joy of heart-wide-open love, but it's safe.

Or is it? Soon, while sitting in this mental bunker, we find that we've not gone to a Safe House after all, but to a Jail House. We see that while we thought we were going to be safe, the people here are always angry and afraid. The energy we were trying to get away from is the energy we feel now more than ever. (Meanwhile, the people who have "escaped" now feel totally secure in the arms of a Larger Love.)

~

You may not be in this jail right now. It is hoped that you are not, that even a bit of what you've read here has brought you sufficient Reminders to get you out of your imprisonment. Yet wherever you are right now, if you look around you, you will notice that most people have not fully understood the phrase "Free Will." Their Current Thought is not combined with their Present Awareness.

You can now always tell if you have slipped back into that place yourself. It is when your Current Thought is not connected to your Eternal Awareness, when your Mind is not combined with your Soul. It is when your Current Thought is negative.

If your thought is a negative one, you are without question coming from your Mind alone. You know this because the Soul, where Eternal Awareness resides, is *incapable of negativity of any kind.* It knows too much. It *is* too much. It is *infinite,* while the Mind is finite.

Current Thought can, of course, also be positive. Not all thought is negative. The Mind can be either negative *or* positive, depending (quite literally) upon the mood of the Moment. The Soul, on the other hand, is incapable of such duplicity.

The Eternal Awareness arising from the Soul will, therefore, never produce negative energy of any kind. Your Mind, on the other hand, can produce an unending supply of it.

Yet stand where the Mind and Soul come *together* and the Soul's positivity converts whatever negativity the Mind may at any Moment hold—using Gratitude, Recontextualization, Compassion, Forgiveness, and Meditation.

These tools cause the sheer uplifting *power* of the positive to supersede the draining energy of the negative. But none of it will happen—*none of it*—without you first entering fully into Willingness.

We can become lighter & lighter.
We can pull from the soundless sound
We can sit completely still in movement.
We can open every cell, as wide as it can open.
How, you say? And I dare say
by Willingness first.
Then faith in the Unbelievable.
By Perseverance beyond your idea of it,
then by layer upon layer of Patience.
Now, Grace moves through, unannounced.
Now, the Unimaginable. Miracles.
Then Darkness. The Womb. Gestation.
Birth. Then Light.

Then Willingness again ...

———

"Willingness"
©2007 em claire

38

A Bit More About Basic Instinct

Dear Companions on the Journey . . .

No human being wants merely to *get by*. We want to rise to the highest expression of ourselves that any moment, and that this entire life, will allow.

We mentioned this before, but let's delve into it a little more deeply, because it is important that you have a full articulation of the driving motivation of your life.

Our Basic Instinct is not survival, but *revival:* The revival of the grandest dream that lives within all of us. The revival of the greatest idea we ever had about ourselves. The revival of the *original truth* that we held about God—which is that God wants only the *best* for us, and gives only the best *to us,* and sees only the best *in us,* and has in *store* for us . . . *nothing but The Best.*

This whole life is not about redeeming ourselves from Original Sin and never has been—it's about reclaiming ourselves with *Original Truth.*

Life is *the best,* and we've made it seem as if Life is *the worst.* God is *the best,* and we've made it seem as if God is *the worst.* Or at least, *the scariest.* The most *judgmental.* The most *vindictive* and *revengeful.* The most *damning* and *condemning* and *punishing.*

Wow. No wonder human beings think it is "good" to be a "God fearing" person. Wow.

Yet we are all as pure as little children, wandering about in innocent confusion, not knowing, not remembering, who we really are; not understanding, and not being told, what is really going on.

We can ignore our Basic Instinct if we want to, but we can't claim it's not there. It lives within all of us. The yearning *by* us for the best *in* us is what motivates all of us. It's what can bring satisfaction to a simple game of *solitaire*, for goodness sake. Or joy to a solo round of golf. Or the overcoming of a bad habit. Or the improving of one's reaction to a challenging person or event.

It's about *beating yourself*, besting your own *last best effort*. It's about being *better than you ever were before*—without there needing to be anyone else around to know about it, much less to compete with.

It's not about competition, it's about REPetition—doing Life over and over and over again until you do better than you ever did *or ever thought you could!*

This is what your life is all about, and *Eternal Life* as well: giving you chance after chance to Best Yourself.

(And please notice—for *God's sake*, please notice—this is *not* the same as doing something over and over again until you "get it *right.*" This is not about being Right or Wrong. This is about being *better and better*. This is about getting closer and closer to Completion.)

~

This fundamental impulse of every human is what we have called, here on these pages, "Divinity"—but you may call it anything you wish. The highest expression of Life. The greatest expression of Self. The grandest expression of Being.

It is, in the end, The Only Thing That Matters because it really *is* What One Desires—the One that is you, and The One that is One *with* you.

It is the only thing people are living for, and, ironically, it is that to which the largest number of people pay the least amount of attention.

And so, you brought yourself the Reminders that you have found here, because now you see that if you didn't *know* about these things—if you hadn't reminded yourself of The Agenda of the Soul, the Sacred Journey, and the Divine Purpose—you would never get away from struggling and suffering; you would never lead a truly joyful, wondrous, exciting and fulfilling life.

Now you see that the intersection of Current Thought and Eternal Knowledge is the crossroad of the Mind and Soul, the junction of Experience and Awareness. The trick is to *stand in the intersection;* to *stay centered;* to feel the combining of The Totality of You; to be submerged in the mix of Body, Mind, and Soul; and by this single decision to live life as a Complete human being.

39

One Last Question, One Last Answer

ALL OF THIS you may have already experienced. It is not as if this book is bringing the possibility of it all to you for the first time. Yet as we have mentioned before, it has been challenging for many people to sustain this connection with the Divine, to remain in that place of *center* between the Mind and the Soul, even *if* they are using the tool of Meditation.

Daily life just keeps getting in the way. Making a ruckus. Causing a stir. And so we come upon a final question: How can we stay "centered" when, in the many moments between our meditation, so-called "real life" *can,* in fact, create an obstacle?

The answer is, you have to find a way to return to that resonant field that you visited during your Meditation and that you experienced as you used those tools of Gratitude, Recontextualization, Compassion, and Forgiveness Forgone that you've been told about here.

With Willingness as the *first* gift you give yourself, you can find that way. You can spontaneously merge what spiritual messenger and visionary Barbara Marx Hubbard calls your "Local Self" and your "Universal Self." There is a resonant field created by the two, where both exist collaboratively, and Barbara says you can *feel* that resonance. In human language, she calls it "love."

Whenever you experience daily life "getting in the way," whenever you find yourself caught up in paying the bills, handling business, keeping everyone happy, meeting the deadline, and doing what you have to do to get through the day—and especially whenever you encounter a person who is being difficult (or you catch *yourself* being difficult)—you may want to do as Barbara does.

"I put my hand over my heart," she says, "until I feel the love."

First, you'll feel love for yourself, then you'll feel love for others, then you'll feel love for Life Itself—and then you'll feel love for All That Is, called Divinity.

You'll feel love for yourself because of all that you are doing, and trying to do, to keep all the plates in the air and to keep all of the promises you've made to yourself, and for the genuinely good person that you know yourself to be at heart.

You'll feel love for others because you'll understand in fullness that the person in front of you is having their own difficult moment, and that others in the world are meeting their own challenges, facing their own dilemmas, and that all of them are totally good at their core, just as you are, wanting only the best, and so unsure of how to produce it.

You'll feel love for Life Itself, for its wonderful process of Reliable Repetition, giving you chance after chance to make the next grandest decision about yourself and create the next grandest experience of your Self.

And you'll fall in love with God because of the magnificence and the wonder and the glory of Divinity—and for *letting you in on it,* for giving you a "piece of the action," for your eternal connection with your Universal Self, and for your Oneness with the Divine.

If you'll give yourself just one tiny moment, close your eyes, take a breath, hold your hand over your heart, and enter the resonance, you'll *feel,* not just conceptualize, that your Body, Mind, and Soul are One, and you'll feel that The Totality of You and The All of Everything are The Same Thing.

But you have to be willing. You have to have given yourself, and received, the gift of Willingness.

～

As you look around you, you will see that many people have not. Their Current Thought is not combined with their Present Awareness, much less the Eternal Knowledge of the Soul, and they might label all of this nothing more than "New Age Gobbledygook."

"God is the answer," some of them may even say—but then they'll insist on making God an angry, violent, and vindictive Deity, giving humans the perfect rationale for being angry, violent, and vindictive with others.

This is not the answer, and this is not the truth about God.

Others say there is no such thing as "God," that traditional religion as well as so-called New Thought spirituality have it wrong, and that there is no resource in the form of Divinity that is open to us for guidance or assistance at any level.

In both cases, this is the biggest error in assessing its reality that Humanity has ever made. There is a single sentence that sums up the entire message of *Conversations with God* in five words. Here is God's message to the world: "You've got me all wrong."

If we have no belief in God, and no belief in the existence of the human Soul, we are left with the limited device of our Mind. It has been stated here repeatedly that this life will make no sense whatsoever to our Mind.

Only with the insight and the wisdom and the eternal clarity of the Soul *added* to the experiential reference points of the Mind can what is occurring in our life, and on this planet, make sense. And only with this combining of the Mind and the Soul can one's perspective be sufficiently enlarged to find hope in what would otherwise be a seemingly hopeless world.

> A Soul Knowing:
> If your thought is a negative one, it is the work of your Mind Alone.

The world stands today in need of healing, in need of help, in need of being re-created, if—and only if—the way it now presents itself is not a reflection of who we are. If we want to keep things the way they are, then the world "needs" nothing. Only if we see a world that does not represent (that is, re-*present*) us do we "need" to regain the immense power that God and our Soul provides for us and use it to alter our experience of life.

It is observable that the largest number of people are not tapped into that power. They have not approached the intersection of Mind and Soul. Some may not even know of this resonant field. Or, if they know it does exist, they may not know how to get there. Or, if they have gotten there, they have retreated to their Mind, because they were familiar with that territory.

The result is that millions of people are holding negative ideas in their Current Thought. You are observing this, no doubt, all around you. You hear, from social networks and public media all over the world, statements such as . . .

Utter disaster is ahead.

Global calamity is on the horizon.

System collapse is inevitable.

Life is nothing but an unending struggle.

Things are only going to get worse.

There is no possibility of anything getting better. None.

I cannot survive any of this and be happy in this world.

I'm not sure I even want to be here.

I'm not sure I even want to live.

Because human beings everywhere find themselves now deeply immersed in this milieu, even some ordinarily optimistic people have begun to gravitate toward those ideas.

And "gravitate" is the right word, because it is a gravitational force that pulls us all downward, so that we see only the gravity of the situation and the grave nature of what we assume to be our only possible future—which would lead anyone to yearn for the grave itself.

Yet you can choose not to gravitate, but to elevate.

You can choose to elevate your thinking, elevate your declarations, and elevate your expectations through elevation of your inner self to your Eternal Awareness, where you clearly see what *Consciousness* is placing before you.

And you see it not as the end of anything, but as the beginning of everything. Certainly, of everything that really matters. For even if the whole of our exterior world does "fall apart"—which is not going to happen—even if our economic systems totally collapse, and our political systems completely cave in, and our religious systems suddenly dissolve, and even if every social system utterly disintegrates, there will still be *us*. And, fascinatingly, we will no longer be separated, because we will *all be in the same boat*.

With the disbanding of our *systems* will come the disbanding of our *separations*. No longer will we see each other as rich or poor, no longer will it matter if we are Democrat or Republican, no longer will the labels conservative or liberal, Christian or Jew, Muslim or Hindu have any separating power. It won't matter if we are black or white, gay or straight, male or female, young or old . . . and we will see, actually—finally *see*—that all these "systems" we had put in place to make it a better world did nothing but *separate* us.

So all that would happen is that our artificial differences would dissolve, our separations would disappear, our imagined "superiority" would be laughingly discarded, and our inability to compromise on even the smallest things would instantly evaporate as we all strived together to build a newer world.

If we came from the wisdom of our Soul, that newer world would likely include this list, as found in *The Storm Before the Calm*:

> 1. An acceptance, at last, of the true identity of all
> humans as an aspect and an individuation of Divinity.

2. The embracing by more and more people—ultimately, millions—of the truth of the Oneness of all life and of humanity.

3. An understanding of why we are here upon the earth—a clarity as to the soul's agenda.

4. An end to abject poverty, to death by starvation, and to mass exploitation of people and resources on the earth by those in positions of economic and/or political power.

5. An end to the systematic environmental destruction of the planet.

6. An end to the domination of our culture by an economic system rooted in competition above cooperation and in the continuing quest for economic growth.

7. An end to the endless struggle for Bigger/Better/More.

8. An end to all limitations and discriminations holding people back—whether in housing, in the workplace . . . or in bed.

9. The providing, at last, of an opportunity—one that is truly equal—for all people to rise to the highest expression of Self.

10. Not the putting into place of adjustments to our social systems for the sake of "social correction," but as a living, on-the-ground demonstration of who we really are and who we choose to be as a species.

We would produce a new kind of leadership on our planet as well. Not leaders who say, "Ours is a better way. Our political philosophy, our religious persuasion, our sexual orientation, is *better* than yours, so follow us!" but rather, leaders who say, "Ours is not a better way, ours is merely another way. But if all walk together, if we all *work* together, if we all *pull* together, we can create a way to *make* things better for *all* of us—black *or* white, gay *or* straight, young *or* old, male *or* female—because we're all in this together. Nothing separates us except that which we allow to stand between us simply because of a thought that we hold in our head—a thought that was probably not even our own experience, but that was picked up from *somewhere else.*

We would find that our differences do not have to produce divisions, our contrasts do not have to create conflicts, our aspirations do not have to generate castigations.

In short, we would create a new way of being human.

40

Let Your Soul Talk to You

DEAR AND GENEROUS FRIEND OF THE SOUL . . . you *are* generous, you know, and you have been generous here, with your time and your patience. You've allowed certain notions here to be restated and repeated, creating emphasis on the points in this exploration that *deserve* emphasis.

There is much of which you have reminded yourself here, and much could have been lost were it touched on only fleetingly. So thank you for that generosity. A final thought, then, is offered here.

~

There are millions of them. Billions of them. *Trillions* of them. They're called Moments. Strung together, they're called a Life.

No single Moment has a prescribed length. It could last one second, one minute, or one hour. Or much longer than that.

Yet there is something unusual, something unique about the Most Important Moments: the longer they are, the shorter they seem; the shorter they are, the longer they seem.

If you've ever spent an evening saying a final good-bye to a dearly loved one, you know that the minutes go by oh, too fast. If you've ever spent even a few seconds looking deeply into your beloved's eyes, you know that time can stand still.

Thus, a few seconds can seem like an hour, and an hour can seem like a few seconds. It is their *content* that produces our experience of their length.

In whatever way they are experienced, however, Moments come and Moments go before you know it, and then they are called Memories. They become etched in your Mind. They are yours for a lifetime, and no one can take you away from you.

Nor can you rid yourself of the ones you don't wish to keep.

Moments that will soon turn into Memories are going on right now, as you're reading this, and through all of them—the slow ones and the oh-too-fast ones, the good ones and the not-so-nice ones, the fun ones and the ones that are boring or dreary—there is only one thing that matters.

Because most people have no idea of what that is, they miss it. Moment after Moment after Moment, they miss it. After a few years they realize this, but by then it's too late. Nothing can be done about the Moments that have passed.

But there's good news here. Something *can* be done about the Moment that's *coming up*. And about the one after that. And the hundreds more that will arrive this day. And the thousands more that will appear this week. And the millions more that will happen this month. And the billions more that will occur this year. And the trillions more that will present themselves before one dies.

Yes, about those something can be done. And as you contemplate *what* you can do about those in your life, and what you *want* to do about those, you will know one thing. What you *don't* want to do is *waste them*. Not anymore. No, not anymore.

~

Beginning now, you can make an inner commitment to have regular "visits" with your Soul. Use the tools offered to you here if you think it might feel good to do so. Go to the place, and come from the place, where your Mind meets your Soul as often as you can. This is the place of Self-Realization to which you are called by The Divine. From this place ideas will seem to be "brought" to you every day. Sometimes you may create it so that it "looks like" these sources are outside of you, and sometimes you will allow yourself to experience that there is Only One Source, and that It is speaking as you from within you.

In particular when you experience the One Source coming from within, keep a record of what you are "hearing;" write down the words you are given. A journal of these insights will prove invaluable to you later—maybe even *moments* later, just a breath after committing them to writing, and in some cases years later, when you will turn to your journal and open it to just the right place at exactly the right time.

In the second part of the Addendum to this book is a small sampling of the kind of messages that can come to you. These may appear—as may this whole book—to have come to you from a Source outside of yourself. They are but an example of what can and will move through you when, with Willingness as your guiding energy, you invite into your Mind your own Soul's wisdom.

~

Our exploration here is now ended—and your own explorations have now just begun, at a new level. Experiment with what you have remembered here. Step into the rich and full living of it.

Truly spiritual people—people who see themselves as more than mere chemical creatures, but as spiritual beings who have placed themselves on Earth for particular and special reasons having to do with much more than simple survival—are aspiring, determined, committed, enterprising, motivated, and deeply purposeful. They want lives "overflowing with significance" (to borrow a wonderful phrase from Karen Armstrong in *The Case for God*).

Look to see if your life is now overflowing with significance or with struggle. Do you see daily events as presenting opportunity or opposition? Is there any possibility that your life would or could change for the better, no matter how "bad" or "good" it might be now?

If you believe that such a possibility does not exist, that life is one travail after the next and that's just the way it is, you have no doubt experienced it that way for a very long time, for you see no connection between your declarations and your demonstrations. Remember this: Life will always make you right.

Yet if you believe that, yes, there is certainly a possibility that life could change for the better, and could become less of a struggle, what do you think could cause that to happen?

"I don't know!" you might cry out. "I've been doing all I can! I've been begging God to help me! But He just keeps piling it on!"

Indeed.

And the suggestion here is that you could view each of life's events and circumstances as "piled on" opportunities for the expression and experience of the grandest part of you—the part of you that is Divine.

You see, if you "beg God for help," that is your announcement that you need it. And your announcement that you need it produces the exact experience it announces. Yet if you do not beg God for help, but *thank* God for helping you already—helping you to fulfill your very purpose for being here—then you *switch the energy in your life completely around.* Encountered in this way, with gratitude, with compassion for yourself, and with deep understanding, every event can be a blessing. You might even make that your new mantra:

Every Event Is a Blessing

There is a miracle awaiting here. The miracle is that this shift of your thinking about what is now occurring—this . . . this *recontextualization* . . . of the moments of your life—can have an effect not only on those very moments, but on your future moments as well. For life is a copying machine, cranking out faithful duplicates of what you put in. If you see today's events not as opportunity, but as opposition, tomorrow's events will prove out your theory. Life wants you to receive what you want to receive, and what you want to receive is announced by exactly what you declare yourself to be receiving now. This brings up the classic question: Which came first, the chicken or the egg? And the answer is: Yes.

Now you can peer deep, deep within that enigma, or you can lose patience and stand outside of it. Yet it is within the enigma of Life that Life's enigma is solved. It is by looking right at the puzzle that the missing piece is found.

But don't believe this simply because it is written here. Watch your own life closely. And, should you choose to recontextualize your experience as we are suggesting here, look to see if you don't at least, if nothing else, find a little more peace.

Then, from this place of greater inner peace, undertake a quiet exploration of how your life's moments might begin to change even further if you were to ask life's key question at every decision-point throughout your day:

> *How does what I am doing right now*
> *serve the agenda of my Soul?*

Once in a while, rephrase the question if it helps. As you find yourself moving through your life busily responding to the day's demands, or perhaps busy reacting to a person or situation that may not seem the most pleasant to you, ask yourself this about your response:

> *What does this have to do with my Sacred Journey?*
> *What part of my Divine Purpose is this serving?*

And finally, at any time during your days and nights, as you look out upon the world and experience yourself within it, you might find it wonderful to softly inquire:

> *How do I choose for Divinity to be expressed*
> *through me in the next grandest way in this moment?*

This much please know right now: You have been richly serving The Agenda of the Soul and The Divine Purpose since you began reading this book. It's been said a number of times, and we'll close by saying it once more: You did not come here by accident. You did not find this book by chance. This does not mean, however, that it was guaranteed you would read it, much less follow its suggestions.

You always, always have Free Choice.

The fact that you made the choice to bring these remembrances to yourself, and to even dance for a while with the idea that you—or a part of you, at least—actually wrote this book, says mountains about who you are, the kind of person you've chosen to be, and the kind of gift you bring to every person in your life.

How lucky they are to know you!

~

Now, as your next expression of Free Will, you are invited to look within and to announce and declare *for yourself* what is The Only Thing That Matters. It has been said here that it is What One Desires, and that What One Desires is for you (and all of Life) to experience the highest expression of Divinity possible in any Present Moment.

Yet there is a higher answer than that. We have waited until this moment to bring it to you. It is an answer far more profound for you, far more true for you, and far more specific to you than anything you have read here so far. You will find that higher answer on the pages that follow.

Oh. A final note. On these pages, as in all of Life, you will find there only what you put there. So you are invited to assume, please, once again, the role of the author of this book. Pick up a pen and please finish this book in your own handwriting, in the exact way that you wish. For in the end, The Only Thing That Matters is what you decide is The Only Thing That Matters. So provide your own answer, in your own words, to the question: What is your truth about What One Desires? This will be a wonderful reference for you days, weeks, months, or even years from now.

Good.

And very good.

So now, always remember—indeed, of all the Remembrances offered here, let this be the one held by you as the most important: You are a blessing.

You have been a blessing to many, many people. You have done more kindnesses, big and small, for more people in your life than you could possibly remember. But those kindnesses *are* remembered. They are imbedded in the hearts of all those who received them from you, and they are written on the wings of all the angels in heaven. It is what makes the angels fly.

Even as you look up in your final moment on Earth, remember this, and then, watch for those angels. For they will fly straight to you, bringing back to you all the energy of every kindness you have ever offered to another. For this is the purest energy, and it is the energy that you will use to go Home.

Yet that is not now. Not in this precise Moment. For now, know that yes, yes, you are The Gift. There is no mistaking that. Your life has been a testimony to that, far more than you could possibly imagine. Yet wait. Just wait until all of your goodness is added up. Then you will be clear. Then you will know what God knows now: you are God's Beloved Other, and you have brought blessings to others every single time you have done a kindness, no matter how small.

Every.

Single.

Time.

And now God is waiting to give you the biggest hug to thank you for this, for blessing the lives of so many others so many times in so many ways, allowing Divinity Itself to be made manifest just as God had planned—on Earth as it is in Heaven.

God will give you that hug right now if you will let God do it. Place you hand over your heart right now. In this, as in all things, God must work through you. So gently place your hand over your heart even as you read this.

Then feel the hug.
There.

There now.

You're Complete.
You're Home.
Without having to go anywhere.
For it is true . . .
Home *is* where the heart is.

May blessings continue to flow to you, and through you, all the days of your life. And flights of angels sing thee to thy rest.

Afterword

The *Conversations with Humanity* series of books places a particular and specific point of view about Life before the people of our world, and then invites input, ideas, and commentary of all kinds about that point of view, so that humanity itself will rewrite its Cultural Story.

It is clear that the story we are now living, individually and collectively, on this planet is not working for the largest number of us (or anything close to it).

If we wish to alter our everyday experience during the time we each spend on Earth, we will find it of enormous benefit to begin paying attention to The Only Thing That Matters. This point has been made repeatedly in the *Conversations with God* series of books, upon which all of the material in this present volume is based—including the message that you have brought this material to yourself, using the metaphysical "trick" of making it seem as if it was written by "someone else."

If you would like to continue your interaction with this larger part of Self that forms the community called humanity on Earth, you may do so on a daily basis at the Internet portal site found at . . .

www.cwgportal.com

There you will have an opportunity to enter into a lively Global Conversation taking place daily around the topics explored here, join with people from across the globe in seeking to create Oneness as a worldwide experience through the work of Humanity's Team, share the life-changing messages you have found here through the CWGforParents home-schooling program, and learn more about how to apply the principles of

Conversations with God in your daily experience through programs of the Conversations with God Foundation and CWG Connect.

Perhaps most important, if you are facing a major life challenge or difficulty right now and would like immediate spiritual assistance or guidance, you will find that, too, at this portal website. Just look for the CWG Healing Community, the ministering service of the Conversations with God global outreach.

A number of years ago a book was given to us called *Home with God: In a Life That Never Ends.* In it, God engaged in a dialogue around what occurs at the end of our present physical life, and thereafter. As part of that exploration, a question was asked about what our world would "look like" if all of us looked more closely at what we know deep inside to be true about ourselves and about Life.

Much of what was offered there relates directly to what has been offered on these pages. As an Afterword to the present text, we offer this excerpt, in which Divine wisdom is brought to us in the words of The Divine. The excerpt addresses an issue that readers such as you have brought up frequently. "I've heard all this before," people say. "Tell me something *new.*"

Here, from *Home with God,* is a response to that in the form of a dialogue between a human being and God.

God speaks first . . .

~

Now you can say that you've heard all of this before—but you are not *acting like it.*

That is why you keep telling yourself this over and over.

What would it "look like" if I *were* "acting like it"?

If I really understood this and didn't need to have this conversation circle back, again and again, over what I "think" I already know, what would that look like?

First, you would never entertain negative thoughts in your mind again.

Second, if a negative thought *did* happen to slip in, you would get it out of your mind immediately. You would think of something else, deliberately. You would simply *change your mind about that.*

Third, you would begin to not only understand Who You Really Are, but to honor and demonstrate that. That is, you would move from what you Know to what you Experience as the measure of your own evolution.

Fourth, you would love yourself fully, just as you are.

Fifth, you would love everyone else fully, just as they are.

Sixth, you would love life fully, just as it is.

Seventh, you would forgive everyone everything. (And now we would add, by not having to forgive anyone at all.)

Eighth, you would never deliberately hurt another human being again—emotionally or physically. Least of all would you ever do this in the name of God.

Ninth, you would never mourn the death of another again, not even for a moment. You might mourn your loss, but not their death.

Tenth, you would never fear or mourn your own death, not even for a moment.

Eleventh, you would be aware that everything is vibration. *Everything.* And so you would pay much more attention to the vibration of everything that you eat; of everything that you wear; of everything that you watch, read, or listen to; and most important, of everything that you think, say, and do.

Twelfth, you would do whatever it takes to adjust the vibration of your own energy and the life energy that you are creating around you if you find that it is not in resonance with the highest knowing you have about Who You Are, and the greatest experience of this that you can possibly imagine.

Excuse me, but how does all that happen? For instance, how can I become "cognizant" of the "vibration" of a piece of clothing, or a meal listed on a menu, to say nothing of something that I'm thinking, saying, or doing?

It's really quite simple. Tune in to how you feel.

Now I can just see someone saying, "Boy, what a piece of new age jargon—*get in touch with your feelings.*"

Those who see it as jargon will experience it as jargon. Those who see it as wisdom will open the door to a whole new world.

Any suggestions on how to do that?

It is just a matter of focus. Most human beings are focused most of the time on things that do not really matter. Yet if they were to take a few moments each day to focus on what does, they could change their whole lives.

(Inserted note—2012: This was given to us in the above dialogue many years ago!)

Your body is a magnificent instrument of highly sensitive energy receptors. Believe it or not, you can run your hand six inches over the food in a buffet line and, without touching it, feel whether it is of benefit to you to eat that right now. You can do the same thing with clothing that you are picking out of a closet to wear for the day, or that you are thinking of buying in a store.

When you are with another person, if you will stop listening to what you are thinking and begin listening to what you are feeling, the quality of your communication with that person will skyrocket—as will the quality of the relationship itself.

When you are confused and perplexed and looking for answers from the universe, if you will just turn off the part of you that desperately wants to figure things out and turn on the part of you that knows it has access to every answer—if you will stop trying to decide what to *do* and start choosing what you wish to *be*—you will find dilemmas dissolving and solutions appearing magically right in front of your face.

As for measuring the vibes of thoughts or words, there are very *few* people, actually, who cannot tell you whether they are feeling light or heavy about thinking or saying something. Most people can assess this pretty quickly.

Yes, but—and here is the where the screw turns—*very few people ever do.* At least, that's my observation. Gosh knows, I certainly don't nearly enough.

Then you may wish to start.

Because you are right: very few people use their intuitive and psychic abilities to go deep within themselves and get in touch with their feelings before they think or say or do something. Very few people even do it afterward. If you did this you would allow yourself to be satisfied with nothing less than lightness. You would have nothing to do with anything that has heavy vibes. You would seek to lighten the vibration of everything that you observe, create, experience, and express. You would call this "enlightenment," and you would see amazing results in a very short period of time.

End of excerpt.

It is the hope that you will hear, loud and clear, the messages that you have brought yourself in the reading you have done here. May you experience God's blessings flowing to you, and *through* you, all the days of your life.

Neale Donald Walsch
Ashland, Oregon
September, 2012

Addendum

NOTE: The material in this section of the Addendum is adapted from its first publication in the book *When Everything Changes, Change Everything* (Hay House, 2010). It offers a look at four different types of Meditation.

~~~

Although there is no one form of meditation that is "better" than another, so-called "sitting meditation" is what many people are most familiar with and want to know more about. So people who seek to make a connection between their Mind and their Soul may wish to undertake the practice of sitting meditation twice a day—15 minutes each morning and 15 minutes each evening.

Try, if it is possible, to set a regular time when you will do this. Then see if you can stick to that time. Yet if you cannot keep such a consistent schedule, know that any time will do, so long as it is at least twice a day, early and late.

When you meditate you may want to sometimes sit outside, if it is nice and warm, allowing the morning sun to bake down upon you or the stars to sparkle above you. Inside, you might sit by a window and let the dawn sun pour in and the night sky enclose you. There is, as has been said, no "right way" to do sitting meditation. One may sit in a comfortable chair, or on the floor, or upright in bed, for that matter. Choose what works for you.

Some people sit on the floor, usually with no backrest but occasionally against a wall or a couch, because floor sitting keeps them more "present" in the space. They report that if they are too completely comfortable, as in an overstuffed chair or on the bed, they tend to doze off or fade away from the moment. When they are sitting on the floor, or outside on the grass, this rarely occurs. They are totally mentally "present."

Once sitting, begin by paying attention to your breathing, closing your eyes, and simply listening to yourself inhaling and exhaling. Be in blackness and pay attention only to what you are hearing. When you have "united"—that's the only word that seems to fit here—with the rhythm of your breath, begin to expand your attention to what your "inner eye" is seeing.

Usually at that point this is nothing but darkness. If you are seeing images—that is, "thinking thoughts" of something and seeing that in your mind—work to fade those thoughts out, like a "fade to black" on the movie screen. Turn your mind to blankness. Focusing your inner eye, peer deeply into this darkness. Be looking for nothing in particular, but simply peering deeply, allowing yourself to search for nothing and need nothing.

For many peoeple what happens next can often be the appearance of what appears to be a small, flickering blue "flame" or a burst of blue light piercing the darkness. Meditators find that if they begin thinking about this cognitively—that is, defining it, describing it to themselves, trying to give it shape and form, or making it "do" something or "mean" something—it disappears immediately. The only way that they can "make it come back" is to pay it no mind.

Many people have to work hard to turn their mind off and just be with the moment and the experience, without judging it, defining it, or trying to make something happen or figure it out or understand it from their logic center. It is rather like making love. Then, too, for the experience to be mystical and magical, most people turn their mind off and just be with the moment and the experience, without judging it, defining it, or trying to make something happen or figure it out or understand it from their logic center.

Meditation is making love to the universe. It is uniting with God. It is uniting with Self. It is not to be understood, created, or defined. One does not understand God; one simple experiences God. One does not create

God; God simply is. One does not define God; God defines one. God IS the definer and the defined. God is the definition itself.

Insert the word Self wherever the word God appears in the above paragraph and the meaning remains the same.

Now, back to the dancing blue flame.

Once you take your mind off it, all the while keeping your focus *on* it, without expectation or thought of any kind, the flickering light may reappear. The trick is to keep your mind (that is, your thought process) off it, all the while keeping your focus (that is, your undivided attention) on it.

Can you imagine this dichotomy? This means paying attention to what you are not paying attention to. It is very much like day dreaming. It is like when you are sitting in broad daylight, in the middle of some place of great activity, and you are paying attention to nothing at all—and to everything all at once. You are expecting nothing and requiring nothing and noticing nothing in particular, but you are so *focused* on the "nothing" and the "everything" that someone finally has to snap you out of it (perhaps by literally snapping their fingers), saying, "Hey! Are you *daydreaming*????"

Usually, one daydreams with one's eyes open.

Sitting Meditation is "daydreaming with your eyes closed." That's as close as I can come to explaining the experience.

Now the dancing blue flame has reappeared. Simply experience it, and do not try to define it, measure it, or explain it to yourself in any way. Just . . . fall into it. The flame will appear to come toward you. It will become larger in your inner field of vision. This is not the flame moving toward you at all, but *you* moving into, and inside of, the experience of *It*.

If you are lucky you will experience *total immersion* in this light before your mind starts telling you about it and talking to you about it, comparing it to Past Data. If you have even one instant of this mindless immersion, you will have experienced bliss.

This is the bliss of total knowing, total experiencing of the Self as One with everything, with the Only Thing There Is. You cannot "try" for this bliss. If you see the blue flame and begin to anticipate this bliss, the flame will disappear instantly, in most reported experiences. Anticipation and/

or expectation ends the experience. That is because the experience is happening in EverMoment, and anticipation or expectation *places it into the future, where you are not.*

Hence, the flame seems to "go away." It is not the light that has gone away; it is you. You have left EverMoment.

This has the same effect on your *inner* eye that closing your *outer* eyes has on your experience of the physical world around you. You quite literally shut it out. Most meditators report that this encounter with bliss comes but once every thousand moments of meditation. Having known it once is both a blessing and, in a sense, a curse, because people are forever wishing for it again.

Still, there can be times when they can retreat from the wishing, remove themselves from the hope, desert their desires, reject their expectations, and place themselves totally in the moment, utterly without anticipation of anything in particular. This is the mental state you may wish to seek to achieve. It is not easy, but it is possible. And if you achieve it, you have achieved mindlessness.

Mindlessness is not the emptying of the mind, but the focusing of the mind *away* from the mind. It is about being "out of your mind"—that is, away from your thoughts for a while. (More on this later.) This gets you very close to that place at the point between realms in the Kingdom of God, the space of Pure Being. This gets you very close to nirvana. This can carry you to bliss.

So . . . if you have managed to find a way to quiet your mind on a regular basis—through Sitting Meditation, what is called Walking Meditation, or "doing meditation" (doing the dishes can be a wonderful meditation, as can reading, or *writing,* a book), or Stopping Meditation (again, I'll get into this more later)—you have undertaken what may be the single most important commitment of your entire life: a commitment to your Soul, to be *with* your Soul, to *meet* your Soul, to *hear* and *listen to* and *interact with* your Soul.

In this way you will move through your life not only from the place of your Mind, but your Soul as well. This is what Ken Wilbur, one of the most widely read and influential American philosophers of our time, refers to in his book *A Theory of Everything* as: Integral Transformative Practice. The basic idea of an ITP, Wilbur says, is simple: "The more aspects of our being that we simultaneously exercise, the more likely that transformation will occur."

That's what we've been talking about here since our conversation began, of course. We've been talking about personal transformation—the altering of your individual experience of all of life. We've been talking about integrating the all three parts of the Totality of You in a cooperating, multifunctioning Whole.

Walking Meditation

The meditation technique described earlier is one way—and one very good way—to go about silencing the Mind and connecting with the Soul. But it is not the only way, nor is it necessarily, for everyone, the best way.

There are many people who find it extremely difficult to sit in silent meditation. For them, it may seem as if the "art of meditation" is something that is lost to them. People who are impatient by nature often found that sitting in silent meditation was not a thing they tolerated well. For them, I suggest Walking Meditation, and everything changes for them around the idea of "meditation." Suddenly, it was something they could *do.*

The first thing that happens when people learned about Walking Meditation is that their whole idea about what meditation *is* completely vanishes, to be replaced by a much more clear and concise picture of what is going on.

For most people, meditation has always meant "clearing the mind of everything," leaving the space for "the emptiness" to appear, so that they could move in consciousness into "the nothingness that is The All . . . " or something like that.

What they were supposed to be trying to do, they thought, was "empty the mind." They were supposed to try to sit in one place, close their eyes, and "think of nothing." This made some people crazy, because their mind never turns off! It is always thinking, thinking, *thinking* of *something.*

So some people never get very good at sitting with their legs crossed, closing their eyes, and concentrating on The Nothing. Frustrated, they hardly ever meditate—and envy those who say they do (although they secretly wondered whether those other folks really did, or simply went through the motions, doing no better than they were able to do).

A story now, please, about a master teacher who once said that most people have entirely the wrong idea of what meditation was about. Meditation, she said, was not about *emptiness,* it was about *focus.* Instead of trying to sit still and think about nothing, she suggested doing a "walking meditation" and moving about, stopping to *focus* on specific things that the eyes light upon.

"Consider a blade of grass," she said. "Consider it. Look at it closely. Regard it intently. Consider every aspect of it. What does it look like? What are its specific characteristics? What does it feel like? What is its fragrance? What is its size, compared to you? Look at it closely. What does it tell you about Life?"

Then, she said, "*Experience the grass in its Completeness.* Take off your shoes and socks and walk on the grass in your bare feet. Think of nothing else but your feet. Focus your attention on the bottom of your feet and consider immensely exactly what you are feeling there. Tell your mind to feel nothing else, just for that moment. Ignore all other incoming data except the data coming from the bottom of your feet. Close your eyes, if this helps.

"Walk slowly and deliberately, allowing each slow and gentle step to tell you about the grass. Then open your eyes and look at all of the grass around you. Ignore all other incoming data except the data about the grass, coming from your eyes and feet.

"Now focus on your sense of smell, and see if you can smell the grass. Ignore all other incoming data except the data about the grass coming from your nose, your eyes, and your feet. See if you can focus your attention in this way. If you can, you will experience the grass as you may never have experienced it before. You will *know* more about grass than you ever knew before, at a deeper level. You will never experience it in the same way again. You will realize that you have been *ignoring the grass* your whole life."

Then, the master teacher said, do the same thing with a flower. "Consider it. Look at it closely. Regard it intently (that is, with *intention*). Consider every aspect of it. What does it look like? What are its specific characteristics? What does it feel like? What is its fragrance? What is its size, compared to you? Look at it closely. What does it tell you about Life?"

Then, she said, "*Experience the flower in its Completeness.* Bring it to your nose and smell it once more. Think of nothing else but your nose. Focus your attention on your nose and consider immensely exactly what you are experiencing there. Tell your mind to experience nothing else, just for that moment. Ignore all other incoming data except the data coming from your nose. Close your eyes, if this helps.

"Now focus on your sense of touch, and touch the flower carefully. Touch the flower at the same time as you smell the flower. Ignore all other incoming data except the data about the flower coming from your fingertips and your nose. Now, open your eyes and look closely at the flower. See if you can still smell the flower, now that it is far enough away for you to look at it and touch it. See if you can focus your attention in this way. If you can, you will experience the flower as you may never have experienced it before. You will *know* more about the flower than you ever knew before, at a deeper level. You will never experience it in the same way again. You will realize that you have been *ignoring the flowers* your whole life."

Then, she said, do the same thing with a tree. Walk over to a tree and consider it. "Look at it closely. Regard it intently. Consider every aspect of it. What does it look like? What are its specific characteristics? What does it feel like? What is its fragrance? What is its size, compared to you? Look at it closely. What does it tell you about Life?"

And she said, "*Experience the tree in its Completeness.* Place you hands upon it and feel it totally. Think of nothing else but your hands. Focus your attention on your hands and consider immensely exactly what you are experiencing there. Tell your mind to experience nothing else, just for that moment. Ignore all other incoming data except the data coming from your hands. Close your eyes, if this helps.

"Now focus on your sense of smell, and smell the tree. Continue touching the tree at the same time as you smell the tree. Ignore all other incoming data except the data about the tree coming from your fingertips and your nose. Now, open your eyes and look closely at the tree. Look up at it, and see if you can climb in consciousness to its top. See if you can still smell the tree, now that it is far enough away for you to look at it. Keep touching it. See if you can focus your attention in this way. If you can, you will experience the tree as you may never have experienced it before. You will *know* more about the tree than you ever knew before, at a deeper level. You will never experience it in the same way again. You will realize that you have been *ignoring the trees* your whole life.

"Now, step away from the tree and lose all physical contact with it. See if you can bring to your mind the experience of the tree as you stand and look at it from farther away. Experience it completely. Do not be surprised if you can smell the tree, even from a distance. Do not be surprised if you can, in a sense, even 'feel' the tree from where you are. What has happened is that you have *opened yourself* to the vibration of the tree. You are 'catching the vibe.' See how far back you can step from the tree and still retain 'contact.' When you lose touch with the experience of the tree, move closer in, move back to it. See if this helps you regain contact.

"This exercise will help you develop your ability to *focus your attention* on whatever you want to *experience at a heightened level.*

"Now, walk. Walk wherever you live. In the country, in the city, it does not matter. Walk slowly, but deliberately. And look around you. Let your eyes fall where they may. As your eyes find something, focus the fullness of your attention upon it. It can be anything. A garbage truck. A stop sign. A crack in the sidewalk, a pebble by the road. Look at it closely, from right where you are. Regard it intently. Consider every aspect of it. What does it look like? What are its specific characteristics? What does it feel like from where you are? What is its fragrance? Can you sense that from where you are? What is its size, compared to you? Look at it closely. What does it tell you about Life?

"Continue your walk. Pick out three things on your walk to consider in this way. This walk should take you at least a half hour. You cannot consider three things fully in less time, at first. Later, you will be able to consider something fully in just a moment, in a nanosecond. But now, you are just practicing.

"This is Walking Meditation, and what you are doing is training your mind to *stop ignoring* everything you are experiencing. You are training your mind to *focus* on a particular aspect of your experience, so that you may experience it completely."

Practice Walking Meditation in this way for three weeks, the master teacher said, and "you will never experience life the same way again." Then, take the final step in Walking Meditation. Walk outside—or inside, for that matter. You can actually walk anywhere. From the bedroom to the kitchen will do. There is plenty to see, plenty to touch, plenty to experience. You can spend three hours with the carpet alone—and this time, she said, "Do not pick out any particular part of what you are seeing or encountering. Try to encounter *all of it*. Seek to embrace *all of it*. Attempt to focus on *all of it at the same time.*

"Take in the Big Picture. Close your eyes at first, if this helps. Smell what you are smelling, hear what you are hearing, feel whatever you are 'feeling' of the space around you. Then open your eyes and add sight. See everything you are seeing, and nothing in particular. See All Of It. Smell All Of It. Feel All Of It. If this begins to overwhelm you, refocus on a Part Of It, so that you do not lose your psychic balance.

"With enough practice, you will soon be able to walk into any space or place and begin to experience All Of It at some level. You will realize then that you have been literally *walking home.* You have heightened your Awareness. You have raised your Consciousness. You have expanded your ability to be Present, fully, in the Moment.

"Now, do this with your eyes closed and while you are sitting down, and you have Silent Mediation. Boom. It is as simple as that."

With that the master teacher smiled. "Then try this with sex," she said. "Once you experience sex in this way, you will never want to experience it any other way again. You will realize that, all your life, *you have been ignoring what is really going on.*"

And she laughed.

Stopping Meditation

Next, some words about Stopping Meditation.

This is one of the simplest, yet most powerful, forms of meditation. The reason it is so powerful is that it can be done anywhere, and it takes very little time. Therefore, it is perfect for busy people "on the go."

Stopping Meditation means just that. It means you stop whatever you are doing for just a moment and pay attention to something about it. You dissect it in that moment, and then look closely at one of its individual pieces.

This is a little bit different from Walking Meditation in that it does not take a half hour or more, as Walking Meditation can take. In Walking Meditation you deliberately take a walk for the deliberate purpose of deliberately focusing on a deliberate experience. In Stopping Meditation you do not use nearly as much time, but you can accomplish the same thing: *focus.*

Stopping Meditation can be used in the midst of a very busy day. *Combined* with Sitting Meditation and Walking Meditation, it can create a powerful Trio of Tools that can dramatically alter your reality and raise your consciousness within a very short period of time. Yet even if used as the only form of meditation, it can be transformative.

Here is how Stopping Meditation works: Decide that six times today (and every day) you will stop whatever you are doing for 10 seconds and look closely and intently at one of its component pieces.

Let's say you are washing the dishes. Stop what you are doing for 10 seconds—just *stop* in the middle of it—and peer deep inside one aspect of what you are doing. Look, perhaps, at the water. See it splashing on the dishes. See if you can count the drops of water on the dish in your hand. Just count the water drops. It is an impossible task, but undertake to do it anyway, just for 10 seconds.

Consider the wonder of the water. Look deeply into it. Peer inside. *Go* inside, in your Consciousness. See what you experience there; see what you find. Just stop for a tiny moment and appreciate that moment in a singular way.

Okay, now the 10 seconds are up. Now pull yourself out of that highly focused reality and back into the larger space of your experience. Don't get "lost" in it. Blink your eyes rapidly, or snap your finger, and literally snap out of it. Then, notice what you experienced for that brief moment.

Now go on with what you were doing. Yet don't be surprised if it takes on a whole new quality.

What you have done is truly appreciate something. To "appreciate" something is to make it larger, to increase it—as property, for instance, appreciates in value. When you use Stopping Meditation, you increase the value of your life. And of life itself. It has been my experience that this inevitably returns me to a place of peace.

In order to remind yourself to do this six times a day you may wish to have a little timer with you, or set your watch to beep. Later, as you get used to doing this, your stopping will come automatically to you. You will do this without having to be reminded.

Walking down the street, you will simply stop for a moment and select a portion of what you are seeing and see it again, in a deeper way. You will know what you already know about that, but you will know it in a deeper way. This is called "knowing again," or re-cognizing. The purpose of all of your life is simply this: to know again, to recognize, what is true, and Who You Really Are.

There are a thousand ways to do this. Maybe you catch a reflection of yourself in a store window. Maybe you see a bus going by. Perhaps you spy a dog on the street or a pebble at your feet. It does not matter what you focus on for those 10 seconds. Just stop for a tiny moment and appreciate that moment in a singular way.

Experience this while making love. Stop what you are doing for 10 seconds, separate the moment into its component parts, select one part of the moment, and peer deeply into it. Maybe it is the look in your beloved's eyes. Maybe it is a sensation you are feeling—or creating. Just stop for a tiny moment and appreciate that moment in a singular way.

Some people report having regular times when they do this, and making love is one of them. Standing in the shower is another. Eating food is another. Pick up a pea from the plate, or a kernel of corn. Consider it.

Appreciate it. Taste it utterly and completely. Your mealtimes will never be the same. Your showers will never be the same. Your lovemaking will never be the same. *You* will never be the same.

This is Stopping Meditation. It takes one minute a day. Sixty seconds, in six individual 10-second installments. Six moments within which you may produce The Holy Experience.

Today, stop what you are doing. Just *stop*. Look deeply into the Moment. If nothing else, just close your eyes and focus on the sound of your own breath. Experience the pure energy of life moving into and through your body. Just for that Moment, listen to yourself breathe. Watch yourself take deeper breaths. Just listening to yourself makes you want to go deeper into the experience—and so you begin to breath more deeply. It is a wonderful thing, an extraordinary thing. Just *stopping* makes you go deeper. Deeper into your experience, deeper into the mind of God.

Recommended Meditation Program

Now here is a meditation program recommended for many people: (1) Walking Meditation in the morning; (2) Stopping Meditation during the day, six times; (3) Sitting Meditation at night.

The purpose of all of these meditations is to create focus. It is about focusing your attention on your experience. The reason for focus: it allows you to be here now. Focusing on Now pulls you out of yesterday and out of tomorrow. You do not exist in those illusions. Your only reality is This Moment, right here, right now.

Peace is found in such awareness. As is love. For peace and love are one and the same, and you become One and The Same when you enter into The Holy Experience.

Practice Stopping Meditation right now. It's simple, and it takes 10 seconds. Right now, just stop. Close your eyes and just . . .

stop.

Did you do it? That wasn't so hard, was it? Now do that five more times today. Just stop everything for 10 seconds, close your eyes, and breathe easily and slowly and restfully . . . and just "be with" the Moment, whatever it is offering.

Now, continue your reading here.

The Who Meditation

There is another wonderful meditative technique called *The Who Meditation*. It works like this. Whenever you are experiencing an emotion that you don't want to experience, just say "Who?"

That's right. Just say to yourself, "Who?" Ask yourself, "Who is here right now? Who is this that is having this experience?"

If you are alone, you can even turn this into a little chant. It can be very powerful. Just take a deep breath and, on the exhale, softly but powerfully chant: "Whooooooooo?" Extend the vowel sound until you are out of breath. Then inhale and do it again. Do it three times. You will have slowed your vibration and the Invisible part of you will have a chance to "show up."

If you are not alone, but with another, or in some public place, you can do this little chant inside your head. Or you can just ask yourself the question I suggested above . . .

"Who is this that is having this experience?"

You can, of course, identify with any one of the number of "yous" that populate your inner world. There is the Little You and the Big You, the Injured You and the Healed You, the Scared You and the Brave You, the Powerless You and the Powerful You, the Worried You and the Confident You. But the hope is that what will happen, now that you've heard all this, is that when you do the Who Meditation you will chant yourself right into an awareness of your larger self, of your *true* self.

You are not a human being. You are not the person named John Smith or Mary Jones. You are not your Body, you are not your Mind, and you are not your Soul. These are things that You have. The You that has these things—The Totality of You that has *given* your Self these things—is far bigger than any of them, and even all of them put together.

The You that you are is God, in Particular Form. You are Deity Individuated. You are an Aspect of Divinity. And so is everyone and everything else.

Meditate on these things, and you will not only know the truth, you will *experience* it. And in that, you will have achieved the purpose of your whole life. You will have reached another moment of Completion.

~

In this section of the Addendum are messages that are sent to you now, seemingly from a Source outside of yourself. It does not matter how you perceive them, as long as you receive them.

Take a look at what you are facing
in this moment, on this very day.
Do you think this is by accident?
These events are designed to give you
a chance to express and experience
who you really are right here, right now.

~

You who are alive in this
extraordinary time are witnessing
a revolution in humanity's consciousness
and its experience of itself. In fact,
you are creating it.

~

*Perhaps the way to meet tomorrow's
challenges is not to use yesterday's solutions,
but to dare to think the previously unthinkable,
to speak the previously unspeakable,
and to try that which was previously
out of the question.*

~

*Change is an announcement
of Life's intention to go on.*

~

*The way to live without fear
is to know that every outcome
in life is perfect—including the outcome
that you fear most, which is death.*

~

*Many people make themselves unhappy
simply by finding it impossible to accept
life just as it is proceeding right now.*

~

*Do you know why you are alive?
To give voice and action and physicality to God.
Everything else is beside the point.*

~

How to have a positive attitude amidst all
that is happening? You have to will it.
You have to see the gift in what is
occurring. And no, that is not always
easy. But it is possible.

⌇

The fastest way to get to a place
of love and concern for all humankind
is to see all humankind as your family.

⌇

Make it your life's mission today
to bring to the attention of another
just how extraordinary they are.
Say it. Say it. Say it.
Their heart is waiting to know that
their own best thought about themselves can be believed.

⌇

Nothing changes the environment like
one person deciding to love another,
no matter what.

⌇

We are not simply biological creatures,
the result of a happenstance of chemical processes,
walking the earth just trying to get through it all
with a minimum of harm to ourselves and others.
We are Creations of the Deity, Products of the Divine,

Individuations of God. We are Singular Expressions
of The Singularity, Essential Elements
of the Essence of Life Itself.

～

The Body thinks it has an agenda that is important,
and the Mind imagines that its agenda
is vital to your survival. But the older you get
the more you realize that it is the Soul's agenda,
and only the Soul's agenda, that matters.

～

There is no such thing
as the "opposite" of Love.
Love is the only energy in our reality
that has no opposite—although
there are many expressions of Love
that look like its opposite.
Only a Master can see they are
all the same . . . and so, only a Master
can understand, and thus not even have to
forgive, that which is done in the name of Fear.

～

You cannot make a mistake,
you can only make a decision
that will be your next important step.

～

*All challenges are a sign of
spiritual strength, and of the
readiness of the Soul
to move on; to evolve
even further.*

(*Publisher's Note:* Each day an inspirational thought, drawn from the messages in *Conversations with God,* is sent to anyone who asks for it by simply subscribing to a service, which is free from *www.cwgportal.com.* The above is a sampling of those daily messages. The more you create such Awareness as coming to you from a place seemingly outside of yourself, the more you will experience it coming to you from a place deep within. Enjoy the messages both ways, for Life informs Life about Life through the Process of Life Itself—and you *are* that process.)

Contact Points

More information on the wonderful material in this book may be found at *www.cwgportal.com*, which, as indicated in the Afterword, is a portal to many extensions of the messages of *Conversations with God*. There is a great deal of resource material at the multiple sites opened by this portal, as well as opportunities to join others around the world in expressing The Only Thing That Matters in on-the-ground situations.

You may find it interesting to watch as a woman from Argentina calls in via Skype with a question about discerning the difference between messages from the Soul and those from the Mind. The video is viewable at . . .

www.TheOnlyThingThatMatters.com/video

More of the poems of Em Claire may be found at *www.EmClairePoet .com*. Her audio recordings are particularly enjoyed by her fans, as they offer her own oral interpretation, adding to the impact of the words themselves. The recordings, as well a gift book, *Silent Sacred Holy Deepening Heart,* from which the poems here have been drawn, are available at her website.

"Go outside and play!"
said God.
"I have given you Universes as fields to run free in!
And here – take this and wrap yourself in it –
It's called: *LOVE*
and it will always, *always* keep you warm.
And stars! The sun and the moon and the stars!
Look upon these often, for they will remind you of your own light!
And eyes . . . oh, gaze into *every* Lover's eyes;
gaze into *every* Other's eyes
for they have given you *their* Universes
as fields to run free in.
There.
I have given you everything you need.
Now go, go, *go outside*
and
play!"

"Go Outside and Play"
©2007 em claire